Christ
in Exodus

Stan K. Evers

Grace Publications

GRACE PUBLICATIONS TRUST
7 Arlington Way
London EC1R 1XA
England
e-mail: editors@gracepublications.co.uk
www.gracepublications.co.uk

Managing Editors:
M. J. Adams and D. Crisp

First published 2010
ISBN 10: 0-946462-82-8
ISBN 13: 978-0-946462-82-7

Distributed by
EP BOOKS
Faverdale North Industrial Estate
Darlington DL3 0PH
England

e-mail: sales@epbooks.org
www.epbooks.org

Printed and bound in UK by JF Print Ltd, Sparkford, Somerset

Christ
in Exodus

*In memory of Albert Smith, of the
Kingsdown Mission, Upper Holloway,
who was my first pastor.*

Contents

1.

Christic in all the Scriptures

The book of Exodus fits within the framework of the OT – God's inerrant Word – and we should see Christ in the OT and in Exodus. The theme of Exodus is redemption and is rooted in Genesis 3:15. What is a type?

Imagine for a moment that a rich aunt willed to you an ornate jewellery box containing some rare diamonds, but no one gave you the key. What use are diamonds inside a locked box? For many Christians, the Old Testament is like a locked chest; they believe it contains priceless treasure, but finding the key is the problem.

Where, then, are the keys to unlock the Old Testament? These keys come in the pages of the New Testament. The Lord Jesus and the apostles often quote the Old Testament and allude to events it describes. One estimate[1] is that there are at least 1600 direct quotations of the Old in the New and several thousand more New Testament passages that allude to Old Testament verses. The New Testament writers build on the foundation of the Old Testament.

It is clear from 1 Peter 1:10-12 and 2 Peter 1:20-21 that Old Testament writers 'were given words from the very mind of God, and were frequently moved to write far more Truth than they appreciated … The inspired writers … studied their own words just as we search the Scriptures today. No doubt they understood what they had written up to a point, but became "Bible students" when they wished to grasp the detailed implication of the message God had channelled through them.[2]

The origin and structure of the Old Testament

Who wrote the Old Testament? The references above show that God used human authors to write his Word. As they wrote, he directed their use of words and guarded them from error. To quote the apostle Paul, 'All Scripture is God-breathed' (2 Tim. 3:16). God's Word is therefore inerrant – it is free from error and always true.

Who was the human author of Exodus? The book itself identifies Moses as the author (17:14; 24:4; 34:27). Furthermore, Jesus attributes this book to Moses, for example, debating with the Pharisees he said, 'For Moses said, "Honour your father and your mother", and "Anyone who curses his father or mother must be put to death"' – these two quotations, cited by Jesus in Mark 7:10, are from Exodus 20:12 and 21:17.[3]

The Old Testament consists of thirty-nine books divided into four groups. The first group (Genesis to Deuteronomy) is known as the Pentateuch (the word means 'five books') or 'the books of Moses'. Secondly, there are twelve books of history: Joshua to Esther. Thirdly, there are five books of poetry: Job to Song of Solomon. The last group consists of seventeen books of prophecy: the five major prophets, Isaiah to Daniel, followed by the twelve minor prophets, Hosea to Malachi.

Jesus alludes to the Jewish summary of the Scriptures in his conversation with the Emmaus road disciples when he told them that 'Everything must be fulfilled that is written about me in the Law of Moses, the Prophets and the Psalms' (Luke 24:44).

The apostle Peter placed Paul's letter on a level with the Old Testament when he wrote, 'His letters contain some things that are hard to understand, which ignorant and unstable people distort, as they do the other Scriptures, to their own destruction' (2 Peter 3:16). Because the New Testament apostles followed in the footsteps of the Old Testament prophets in writing 'the holy Scriptures', we may use the apostles' writings to interpret those of the Old Testament.

The purpose and theme of the Old Testament

Why did God give us the Old Testament, and is there a central theme running through the thirty-nine books? Paul tells us that 'the holy Scriptures ... are able to make you wise for salvation through faith in Christ Jesus.' He affirms that God's Word 'is useful for teaching, rebuking, correcting and training in righteousness, so that the man of God may be thoroughly equipped for every good work' (2 Tim. 3:16-17). The Old Testament ('the holy Scriptures') show us how to become Christians ('salvation through faith in Christ Jesus'), how to live as Christians ('teaching, rebuking, correcting and training in righteousness') and how to serve the Lord ('thoroughly equipped for every good work'). The Bible – both Testaments – is a book about salvation, sanctification and service. We cannot experience salvation, make progress in sanctification, or serve God apart from Christ.

Paul writes about the purpose of the Old Testament, not only in his letter to Timothy, but also in his longer epistle to the Romans, 'For everything that was written in the past was written to teach us, so that through endurance and the encouragement of the Scriptures we might have hope' (Rom. 15:4). The apostle makes a similar point in his letter to the Corinthians, 'Now these things occurred as examples to keep us from setting our hearts on evil things as they did' (1 Cor. 10:6). His words are in the context of events recorded in the book of Exodus that teach us about Christ the Rock.

How does the Old Testament relate to the New?

The Bible divides into two major sections: The Old Testament and the New Testament. The word 'testament' means 'covenant' – this word sums up the message of the Bible. 'It is the covenant of grace, the covenant in which God pledges salvation to his people on the basis of Christ's atoning death.'[4]

What is the message of both Old and New Testament? It is that salvation is through faith in Christ alone. In the Old Testament, God saved believers through faith in the Christ of prophecy; from New Testament times onwards, God saves believers through faith in the Christ of history. Salvation in both dispensations is through faith in Christ alone. 'It cannot be stressed too strongly that God has always had only one plan of salvation and that is through his Son. The Old Testament is not, therefore, the record of God trying to save people in one way (the law of Moses) and the New Testament the record of him trying another way (Christ). The people in the Old Testament era were saved in exactly the same way as we are, that is, through faith in Christ. The only difference is that they looked forward in faith to what Christ would do, while we look backward to what he has done.'[5]

In reading the Old Testament, we must bear in mind, the doctrine of 'progressive revelation' – God reveals spiritual truth gradually in his Word. Truths hinted at in the earlier parts of the Bible, such as the doctrine of the Trinity, are more fully explained in later books until we reach the full revelation of the New Testament. The Old Testament is incomplete without the New Testament. We read in Colossians that the rituals of the Old Testament are 'a shadow of the things that were to come; the reality, however, is found in Christ.' The writer to the Hebrews echoes Paul, 'The law is only a shadow of the good things that are coming – not the realities themselves' (Col. 2:17; Heb. 10:1). These verses are crucial for our understanding of the Old Testament, especially the books of the Pentateuch.

Christ in the Old Testament

Christ is at the heart of the Old Testament. But how do we see Jesus Christ in the Old Testament without resorting to bizarre allegorical interpretations? We are to compare one Scripture with another, using the fuller revelation of the New Testament to interpret the Old Testament, keeping in mind the central biblical topic of salvation through Christ's death on the cross.

Talking to the distressed Emmaus Road disciples the Lord Jesus 'beginning with Moses and all the prophets, … explained to them what was said in all the Scriptures concerning himself' (Luke 24:27). Later that same day, Jesus suddenly appeared to the fearful disciples and 'said to them "This is what I told you while I was still with you: Everything must be fulfilled that is written about me in the Law of Moses, the Prophets and the Psalms." Then he opened their minds so they could understand the Scriptures' (Luke 24:44-45). On an earlier occasion Jesus said to his Jewish critics 'If you believed Moses, you would believe me, for he wrote about me' (John 5:46). Paul, defending himself before King Agrippa, said 'I am saying nothing beyond what the prophets and Moses said would happen – that the Christ would suffer and … rise from the dead' (Acts 26:22-23). All the roads of the Old Testament – including the book of Exodus – lead to the Lord Jesus Christ. We have divine authority to find Christ in the Old Testament.

Having set the book of Exodus into the context of the Old Testament, we can now move towards seeing Christ in Exodus. Some words of Robert Sheehan point us in the right direction. 'The importance of Moses in the Old Testament is not likely to be overstated … Moses stands as the mediator of the Old Covenant in the same way as our Lord Jesus is the mediator of the New Covenant. Law came through Moses; grace and truth came through Jesus Christ (John 1:17; 2 Cor. 3). Of course, there is a distinction: Moses is God's servant; Jesus is God's Son.'[6]

The link between Genesis and Exodus

The book of Exodus is rooted in the first gospel promise in Genesis 3:15, 'And I will put enmity between you and the woman, and between your offspring and hers; he will crush your head, and you will strike his heel.' Who is the 'offspring' – 'seed' (NKJV) – predicted in this text? The apostle Paul identifies the woman's offspring as the Lord Jesus Christ in Galatians 3:16: 'The promises were spoken to Abraham and to his seed. The Scripture does not say "and to seeds", meaning many people, but "and to your seed", meaning one person, who is Christ.' He came to earth through a virgin birth to defeat Satan and to deliver his elect from the devil's power. Genesis 3:15 predicts Christ's defeat of Satan on the cross. To conquer Satan, the conqueror is wounded and crushed.

Michael Bentley explains the connection between the first two books of the Bible: 'While the book of Genesis tells us of the call of Abraham and the story of his descendants, Exodus describes God's choice of a people for his special possession and the establishment of an acceptable system of worship of his great and holy name. The foundation for the concepts of priesthood, the temple … and the means whereby God's people can approach their holy God are also laid down in this second book of the Bible.'[7]

However, there are some interesting contrasts between Genesis and Exodus. In Genesis, we read the history of a family whereas Exodus relates the history of a nation. The descendants of Abraham are few in Genesis but are numerous – probably about two million – in Exodus. In Genesis, the Hebrews are welcomed and honoured in Egypt but in Exodus, they are hated and feared. In the first book, there is a Pharaoh who declares to Joseph, 'God has made all this known to you'; in the second book, we read about a Pharaoh who declares 'Who is the LORD, that I should obey him and let Israel go? I do not know the Lord' (Gen. 41:39; Exod. 5:2). Genesis ends with Joseph in a coffin and Exodus closes with God's glory descending on the tabernacle in the wilderness.

The theme of Exodus

Exodus is clearly a book about redemption. God says to his people 'I will free you from being slaves ... I will redeem you.' Moses sings, after crossing the Red Sea, 'In your unfailing love you will lead the people you have redeemed' (Exod. 6:6; 15:13). What is redemption? 'The language of redemption is the language of purchase and more specifically of ransom, and ransom is the securing of a release by the payment of a price ... Ransom presupposes some kind of bondage or captivity, and redemption, therefore, implies that from which the ransom secures us.'[8]

Redemption involves a cost; a ransom price is paid. Philip Eveson suggests that there are three aspects to this cost – all pointing us to Christ the Redeemer.[9] Firstly, the arm of Lord: 'I will redeem with an outstretched arm and with mighty acts of judgement' (Exod. 6:6). God exerted great power to redeem the Israelites. His 'mighty acts of judgement' – the plagues – were an expression of divine judgement and showed God's power over Pharaoh and the gods of Egypt (Exod. 7:3-4; 12:12; 15:11; 18:11). The Lord Jesus Christ is the suffering Servant who redeems his people at great cost to himself as is evident from Isaiah 53. Secondly, the Passover sacrifice: the death of the lambs on Passover night was the ransom price paid to release the Israelites from God's judgement. Redemption was accomplished by the death of the lamb whose blood was daubed on the doorframes of each Israelite house. God said 'When I see the blood, I will pass over you. No destructive plague will touch you when I strike Egypt' (Exod. 12:13). Christ is our Passover Lamb, we are redeemed by his blood (1 Cor. 5:7; Eph. 1:7; 1 Peter 1:18-19). Thirdly, the Lord said that 'the first offspring of every womb among the Israelites belongs to me, whether man or animal' (Exod. 13:1-2; see also verses 11-16). However, the Lord took the Levites 'in place of the first male offspring of every Israelite woman'. God said 'The Levites are mine, for all the firstborn are mine ... in Israel, whether man or animal. They are to be mine, I am the LORD' (Num. 3:13). Because the number of firstborn sons exceeded the number of Levites, five shekels per person were paid to redeem the extra boys. This procedure anticipates Christ, becoming the substitute of God's people; he came 'to give his life as a ransom for many' (Mark 10:45; see also Isa. 53:5-6). 'Christ's redeeming blood is of infinite worth and has effected eternal redemption for the countless myriads of God's people from every tribe and nation.'[10]

Old Testament types

We will see in the book of Exodus types of the Lord Jesus Christ. What is a type? The word comes from Romans 5:14, where we read about 'Adam, who was a pattern of the one to come'. 'Pattern' is translated as 'type' in the New King James Version and as 'similitude' in the Authorised Version.[11] In Romans 5, the apostle Paul compares and contrasts Adam and Christ. Biblical scholars debate the definition of the term and what is, or who is, a type. In this book, I am going to use Dr. Peter Master's definition as a guideline: 'Types are persons or objects or events that serve as prophetic illustrations or likenesses of New Testament fulfilments.'[12]

Unlocking the treasure

My aim in this book is to use the New Testament keys to unlock the treasure chest of Exodus. I want you to see in the book of Exodus the Lord Jesus Christ, the Pearl of Great Price. To change the metaphor, I want you to see Christ's portrait in the second book of God's Word so that you will marvel at the wonder of his redeeming love and so that you will want to devote your life to serving him.

So then, let's take the keys and unlock the chest…

2.

Christ the Redeemer
———— (Exod. 1-3) ————

The Hebrews' slavery is a picture of sinners as slaves of Satan. Only God can deliver from slavery and defeat Satan, who is more powerful than Pharaoh. God, who protected the baby Moses and equipped him to rescue the Hebrews, protected and equipped his Son, to bring salvation to his elect. Moses' decision to leave the riches of Egypt is compared with Christ's decision to leave the glory of heaven (Phil. 2). God's dealings with his people in both the Old and New Testaments are rooted in his covenant.

What is the meaning of the word 'Exodus'? It means 'going out' or 'departure' – the book of Exodus tells the story of the enslaved Hebrews' departure from Egypt. What had brought the Israelites from Canaan, the land that God had given to the patriarchs, into Egypt? The opening verses of Exodus answer that question. The elderly Jacob and his family left famine-stricken Canaan and travelled to Egypt, where his second youngest son Joseph, once a slave, had risen to a prominent position so that he was almost as powerful as the Pharaoh. Hearing about the plight of Joseph's family, the Pharaoh had invited them to settle in Egypt. God said to Jacob, 'Do not be afraid to go down to Egypt, for I will make you into a great nation there' (Gen. 46:3). Unknown to Jacob, momentous events would result

17

from his move to Egypt that led eventually to the birth and death of Jesus the Messiah.

Growth

The seventy people who went down into Egypt increased during 430 years to a vast number, fulfilling God's promises to Abraham and to Jacob (Exod. 1:7; Gen. 12:2; 35:11; 46:3). The new Pharaoh 'who did not know about Joseph' saw this growth as a threat to national security (Exod. 1:8). Surely everyone knew about Joseph, who saved his nation from starvation? However, the words 'came to power in Egypt' (Exod. 1:8) may suggest that the new king came from another nation that had conquered Egypt. He was alarmed because of the Hebrews' increasing power, and maybe he was jealous that they occupied Goshen, one of the most fertile areas of Egypt.

Misery

The new king issues three commands. Firstly, he commands the taskmasters to make the Hebrews work harder (1:11-14). Pharaoh forces the Hebrews to become slaves to build the two great store-cities of Pithom and Rameses. Busy slaves are exhausted slaves and therefore less of a threat. Perhaps the king thought that the hard labour would kill the slaves. How wrong he was! The harder they worked the more they increased. Secondly, Pharaoh ordered the midwives to kill every baby boy (1:15-21). The God-fearing midwives, under the leadership of Shiphrah and Puah, ignore Pharaoh's command. 'Were they going to carry out the orders of a powerful king who could destroy them at the least provocation? Or were they going to obey an invisible God who appeared to have done nothing to keep them from trouble while they were in Egypt? In fact, they do not seem to have had any difficulty in deciding whose authority they were going to obey.'[1] We read that 'they let the boys live' (1:17). How do they explain this disobedience to the king? '[The Hebrews] give birth before [we] arrive' (1:19). Does God condone lies? Perhaps the statement was true. 'We can only conclude that their words were necessary in order to protect the helpless Hebrews in the hands of a cruel oppressor.'[2] God rewarded the midwives with families of their own (1:21) – God honours those who honour him (1 Sam. 2:30). Thirdly, Pharaoh commanded all the people to throw every boy into the Nile (Exod. 1:22). No boys would mean that Israelite girls would have to marry Egyptian boys and so the Israelite nation would lose its separate identity. Hebrew parents were to offer their sons as sacrifices to the River Nile, which was regarded as a god by the Egyptians.

Moses tells us that 'The Israelites groaned in their slavery and cried out, and their cry for help because of their slavery went up to God. God heard their groaning and he remembered his covenant with Abraham, with Isaac and with Jacob. So God looked on the Israelites and was concerned about them' (2:23-25). Israel's misery moved the heart of the compassionate God – and so does the plight of sinners.

The distressed Jews did not know that God had already planned their deliverance and was working in the life of Moses, their future deliverer. In the same way, God planned before time that his Son, the Lord Jesus Christ, should come to earth to redeem enslaved sinners (Acts 2:23; Gal. 4:4-5; 1 Peter 1:18-20).

Spiritual slavery

Jesus said that sinners are in a worse kind of slavery: 'I tell you the truth, everyone who sins is a slave to sin.' Sin's slaves serve Satan; they are in 'the trap of the devil, who has taken them captive to do his will'. Sinners serve the 'god of this age' who 'has blinded the minds of unbelievers, so that they cannot see the light of the gospel of the glory of Christ, who is the image of God' (John 8:34; 2 Tim 2:26; 2 Cor. 4:4).

The Hebrews groaned because of their captivity; sadly, many sinners do not realise their plight. However, God hears all who 'cry for help because of their slavery'; his tender heart cannot turn away the penitent. Jesus said 'Whoever comes to me I will never drive away' (Exod. 2:23; John 6:37). The slaves could not release themselves from captivity; neither can we release ourselves from sin's grasp. God who delivered his people from Pharaoh sets us free from Satan's clutches. God alone can redeem his people and our redemption comes with the price tag of Christ's blood.

Protection

Imagine Jochebed's happiness when she became pregnant but those emotions must have been very mixed when she gave birth to a boy (Exod. 2:1-2; 6:20). The writer to the Hebrews comments on the faith of Jochebed and her husband Amram: 'By faith Moses' parents hid him for three months after he was born, because they saw he was no ordinary child, and they were not afraid of the king's edict' (Heb. 11:23). What is the meaning of the words 'no ordinary child'? Moses states that his parents 'saw that he was a fine child' (Exod. 2:2). It means that 'they knew that God had a special destiny for this child. They believed that great things lay in store, and took steps to preserve his life. This involved a fearful risk.'[3] The words 'were not afraid of the king's edict' (Heb. 11:23) tell us 'they knew that their God was far more powerful than any earthly ruler.'[4] Both Jochebed and Amram, from the priestly tribe of Levi, remained faithful to the God of their fathers when most Hebrews worshipped the gods of Egypt (Ezek. 20:6-8). Will you remain loyal to God in these evil days?

Moses' parents placed their three-month old son in a basket 'coated with tar and pitch' to keep the water out and to keep it afloat, and put it 'among the reeds' to stop it being washed downstream. No Egyptian would expect to find an Israelite baby hidden in the Nile, the place of execution.

The parents could easily reach the child and take him out for nourishment. They trusted their vulnerable baby to the care of God, the heavenly Father, and to the watchful, though hidden, eyes of his sister Miriam (Exod. 2:3-4). Sometime later Miriam came rushing home with the news that Pharaoh's daughter had found her baby brother and that she wanted a Hebrew nursemaid for the child; so once again Jochebed held her son in her arms – this time with the authority of Pharaoh's daughter! (2:5-10).

Why should Pharaoh's own daughter protect this child and adopt him as her own son? Perhaps she did not agree with her father's edict but, whatever her reason, her protecting Moses was God's plan to rescue his people. She named the baby Moses – 'drawn out' (verse 10). The baby drawn out of the water would one day draw the Israelites out of slavery in Egypt and lead them to the promised land.

Moses was 'no ordinary child'; Jesus was an extraordinary child, God's eternal Son, God in human flesh walking on earth. How did Jochebed realise that Moses was different from other children? We don't know. Jesus' mother, the Virgin Mary, learnt about her son's miraculous conception from the angel Gabriel: 'You will be with child and give birth to a son, and you are to give him the name Jesus. He will be great and will be called the Son of the Most High' (Luke 1:31-32). An angel visited Joseph to explain the pregnancy of his future wife and identified her unborn child as Immanuel – God with us – predicted long ago by the prophet Isaiah (Matt. 1:18-23; Isa. 7:14). The angels told both Mary and Joseph to call their son Jesus – his name explains the purpose of his birth – 'he will save his people from their sins' (Matt. 1:21). He came to redeem God's elect from sin's slavery.

God, who protected Israel's redeemer from Pharaoh, protected his Son, the divine Redeemer, from the malice of Herod. Wise men asking, 'Where is the one who has been born king of the Jews?' threw King Herod into a panic. He asked the Magi to report to him when they had found the newborn king on the pretext of wanting to worship him. To protect his Son, God warned the wise men, through a dream, to return home by another route. Their failure to appear in Jerusalem led to Herod's order to 'kill all the boys in Bethlehem and its vicinity' aged two or under. God was one-step ahead of Herod; he had told Joseph in a dream, 'Get up, take the child and his mother and escape to Egypt. Stay there until I tell you, for Herod is going to search for the child to kill him.' Matthew sees this escape to Egypt as a fulfilment of Hosea's prophecy, 'Out of Egypt I called my son' (Matt. 2:1-18; Hosea 11:1).

Preparation

The Bible is silent about the childhood of both Moses and Christ. We can be sure that Jochebed and Mary taught their children God's Word. Stephen sums up the first forty years of Moses' life and Luke writes about Jesus' development from a child to a man (Acts 7:22; Luke 2:40,52). God used these 'hidden years' as Moses' initial training to free Israel from Egypt and for Christ's preparation to free his elect from Satan and sin.

Stephen, in his address to the Sanhedrin, said: 'Moses was educated in all the wisdom of the Egyptians and was powerful in speech and action' (Acts 7:22). 'The wisdom of the Egyptians' included reading, writing and mathematics besides music and archery. Moses was 'powerful in speech' despite his protest that 'I have never been eloquent ... I am slow of speech and tongue' (Exod. 4:10). The words 'powerful in ... action' suggest that Moses was a great soldier. Stephen also comments on the incident related in Exodus 2:11-15 – Moses killing an Egyptian – that led to his leaving Egypt. 'Moses thought that his own people would realise that God was using him to rescue them, but they did not' (Acts 7:25). The Hebrews did not recognise their deliverer and years later, the Jewish race rejected their God-sent Redeemer: 'He came to ... his own, but his own did not receive him' (John 1:11). The Sanhedrin stoned Stephen; they had already nailed Jesus to a cross.

We have seen how God started to train Moses; how did he equip Christ of whom Moses is a type? 'And the child grew and became strong; he was filled with wisdom, and the grace of God was upon him ... Jesus grew in wisdom and stature, and in favour with God and men' (Luke 2:40,52). Hendriksen comments, 'The *development* of this child was therefore perfect and this along every line: physical, intellectual, moral, spiritual; for from beginning to end progress was unimpaired and unimpeded by sin, whether inherited or acquired. Between the child Jesus and his [heavenly] Father there was perfect harmony, limitless love ... the young boy Jesus reveals his closeness to his Father.' On the words 'in favour with God and men', he writes, 'He continued to experience increasingly the lovingkindness of his Father and also the friendliness of the people.'[5] To die for men and women, Christ must have a physical body and share our human nature. He came to earth as God in human flesh!

Decision

Following the killing of the Egyptian, Moses fled to Midian. Exodus 2:14 mentions Moses' fear. Was he afraid of relatives or friends of the murdered man seeking revenge? Hebrews 11:27 makes it clear that Moses did not fear Pharaoh: 'By faith he left Egypt, not fearing the king's anger.' Leaving Egypt was an expression of his faith prompted by his deliberate refusal 'to be known as the son of Pharaoh's daughter' and his decisive choice of suffering 'along with the people of God rather than to enjoy the pleasures of sin for a short time.' He exchanged Egypt's treasures for Christ's disgrace (Heb. 11:24-26) and chose to suffer as the redeemer of Israel.

Our Redeemer made a bigger sacrifice than Moses. He willingly chose to leave the presence of the divine King, his heavenly Father, with whom he had enjoyed unbroken fellowship, to suffer with, and for, the people of God. He exchanged heaven's glory for a cross of shame. We learn from Paul's profound statement about Christ in Philippians 2:6-8 that 'from the infinite sweep of eternal delight in the very presence of his Father he willingly descended into the realm of misery, in order to pitch his tent for a while among men. He, before whom the seraphim covered their faces (Isa. 6:1-3; John 12:41), the Object of most solemn adoration, voluntarily descended to the realm where he was "despised and rejected of men, a man of sorrows and acquainted with grief" (Isa. 53:3).' [6]

Covenant

Why did God redeem the Israelites? Because of his love rooted in his covenant. 'God heard their groaning and he remembered his covenant with Abraham, with Isaac and with Jacob' (Exod. 2:24). The 'covenant' means his unbreakable promises made to the patriarchs. What promises did God make to Abraham?
1. Abraham's descendants would become a great nation (Gen. 12:2; 18:18).
2. These descendants would possess the promised land (Gen. 12:7; 13:14-15; 15:18-21; 17:8).
3. These descendants would be God's own people: 'I will be their God' (Gen. 17:8).
4. These promises bring blessing to 'all peoples on earth' (Gen. 12:3; 17:4-6; 22:17-18). Abraham was the father of non-Israelite nations who did not share directly in the covenant, for example, the descendants of his son Ishmael (Gen. 25:12-18) and those of Esau, the Edomites (Gen. 36:1-43). It is clear from Paul's statement in Romans 4:16-18 that this promise means that non-Jews were included in the blessings. God's elect will come from 'every nation, tribe, people and language' (Rev. 7:9).
5. These promises extend to the spiritual descendants of Abraham, the church comprised of Jews and

Gentiles. The true children of Abraham have the faith of Abraham (Gen. 12:3; 17:4-6; 18:18; Rom. 4:16-18). God fulfils these promises in Christ – Abraham's Seed (Compare Gen. 12:7; 13:15 with Gal. 3:16). At the heart of God's covenant is his promise, 'I will be their God' (Compare Gen. 17:8 with 2 Cor. 6:16,18 and Rev. 21:3).

Why did God choose Israel and make them a great nation? Why does he choose his elect from among the nations of the world? Because he is a God of sovereign grace! (Gen. 12:1-3; Deut. 7:7-9; Eph. 1:3-7).

God's time

Forty years passed before God's time arrived for Moses to deliver the Hebrews; thirty years passed before Jesus began his public ministry which reached its climax with his death on the cross; there he paid the price of redemption for his people. Both the ministry of Moses and of Jesus fulfilled God's eternal purposes in God's own perfect time.

3.
Christ is Lord
—— (Exod. 3) ——

'The angel of the LORD*', who spoke to Moses from the bush, is both God and God's messenger. Comparing Exod. 3 with Exod. 23:20-23, we may say that Christ spoke to Moses at the bush. The Angel calls himself, 'I* AM THAT *I* AM*'. Exod. 3:14 links to Matt. 22:31-32, John 8:58, Heb. 1:1-3,10-12 that focus on Christ's deity. Jesus took up the 'I* AM*' title in his seven 'I am sayings' in John's gospel – these sayings teach us about the character of Christ the Lord.*

J ust another day, much the same as any other day during the past forty years, caring for the sheep of his father-in-law Jethro in the hot, lonely desert – so the eighty-year old Moses thought as he left Zipporah his wife. However, this day became a turning point in his life. God spoke directly to him!

Working day after day in the desert, 'Moses would have had time to meditate upon the wonders of God. As he looked around him and saw the majesty of the desert landscape and the mountains, his heart must have been filled with awe, and with love to the God who made all these things. In the desert he would have learned to bow in humble adoration before the Lord.'[1] Perhaps Moses' thoughts went back forty years to his foolish attempt to rescue a Hebrew from a bullying Egyptian by killing him and burying him in the sand; that murder, once discovered, was what had caused Moses to run for his life to Midian (Exod. 2:11-22).

The shepherd

The man raised as Pharaoh's daughter now serves as a shepherd, a despised occupation in the estimation of Egyptians (Gen. 46:34). 'To a man, who judges primarily on the things of the flesh, Moses appears, at this stage in his life, to be a tragic figure. He has lost his position of power and authority, his fame and his riches. And he is now carrying out the most menial type of work in a barren land! [... but ...] here is a poor shepherd who will one day be the deliverer of Israel. In fact, this lowly work is preparation for the task of shepherding the flock of the Lord.'[2] Moses waited patiently for God to deliver his people in his own time and in his own way; God's time had now arrived. Now God came down to rescue his suffering people 'from the hand of the Egyptians and to bring them up out of that land into a good and spacious land, a land flowing with milk and honey' (Exod. 3:8).

In caring for Jethro's sheep, Moses is a type of Christ, the divine Shepherd. He is the *good* Shepherd who keeps his sheep safe in his nail-pierced hands (John 10:11-29). He is also the *great* Shepherd who died and rose again to make his sheep holy (Heb. 13:20-21). Furthermore, he is the *chief* Shepherd who commands elders to 'Be shepherds of God's flock that is under your care, serving as overseers' and who promises 'the crown of glory that will never fade away' (1 Peter 5:2,4). In heaven, the divine Shepherd will lead his sheep 'to springs of living water' and 'wipe every tear from their eyes' (Rev. 7:17).

A burning bush

Coming back to Exodus 3, we read that Moses heard a voice speaking from a burning bush! Bushes often caught fire in the desert, but this blazing bush 'did not burn up' (Exod. 3:2).

Imagine his surprise when he heard the Lord calling 'Moses! Moses!' He answered, 'Here I am.' The Lord said 'Do not come any closer ... Take off your sandals, for the place where you are standing is holy ground' (verses 3-5). Sinful Moses knelt in the presence of the holy God. 'He had to remove his footwear, so that the dirt which had collected on their soles would not soil the place where the Lord God Almighty especially displayed his presence.'[3]

Why did God speak to Moses from within a burning bush? Fire is often a sign in the book of Exodus of God's presence among his people: for example we read in chapter 24:17, 'To the Israelites the glory of the LORD looked like a consuming fire.'[4] The writer to the Hebrews says that even in the new dispensation 'our God is a consuming fire'; we only worship him 'acceptably' when we approach him with 'reverence and awe' (Heb. 12:28-29).

Moses was delighted to hear that God had 'seen the misery' of his people and that he had 'come down to rescue them from the hand of the Egyptians'; he was not so pleased to hear that he was God's chosen deliverer (Exod. 3:6-13). Moses felt inadequate for this daunting task, so God reassured him with a promise, 'I will be with you' (verse 12).

The angel of the LORD[5]

Who spoke to Moses from the bush? 'The angel of the LORD appeared to him in flames of fire from within a bush' (Exod. 3:2). The angel speaks as God – 'God, called to him from within the bush' (verse 4) – and yet he is 'the angel of the LORD', he speaks as God's messenger. Who is 'the angel of the LORD' who is mentioned four times (possibly five) in the book of Exodus? (3:2; 14:19; 23:20; 32:34; cf. 33:2[6]). He is a pre-incarnate appearance of Christ – this is a *theophany*.

Robert Sheehan explains the word 'theophany': 'The combination of the Greek words *"theos"* and *"phanein"* meaning "God" and "to appear" respectively, define a theophany as "an appearance of God".[7] Commenting on 'the angel of the LORD' he says, 'This angel is distinguished from other angels because he speaks as God, delivering his message in the first person singular, and himself promises to fulfil his Word (Gen. 16:10; 22:12). In delivering his message, he is described variously as "the Angel of the LORD" and "the LORD" himself, suggesting an identification of the two (Judg. 6:11,12,14,16,20). Those to whom the Angel of the LORD appeared responded to him and worshipped him as God himself (Gen. 16:13-14; Judg. 6:24). Nor is there any hesitancy on the part of the Angel of the LORD in receiving worship that God alone should receive, a hesitancy elsewhere specifically recorded when mere angels are involved (Rev. 22:8-9).'[8]

Exodus 23:20-23 confirms that 'the angel of the LORD' is Christ. God sends his angel to protect his people on their journey to the land he has prepared for them. God tells them to 'Pay attention to him and listen to what he says. Do not rebel against him; he will not forgive your rebellion since my Name is in him. If you listen carefully to what he says and do all that I say, I will be an enemy to your enemies and will oppose those who oppose you.' The angel forgives sins, which is a divine prerogative (Mark 3:1-12). The angel's words are God's words; the Israelites listened to him to do what God said. 'My Name is in him' means that he is God (compare John 14:9-10). Christ leads believers to the place he has prepared for them. God says that Christ is his Son and we are to 'listen to him' (Luke 9:35).

'I AM WHO I AM

The angel of the Lord, at the burning bush, calls himself 'I AM WHO I AM': 'God said to Moses, "I AM WHO I AM. This is what you are to say to the Israelites: "I AM has sent me to you"' (verse 14). The 'I AM' is the God of your fathers – the God of Abraham, the God of Isaac and the God of Jacob' (verses 13,15). It is usual to pronounce 'LORD' as Jehovah or

Yahweh but in fact we do not know the Jewish enunciation because they concluded from Leviticus 24:16 that it was blasphemous to speak God's name. They used 'LORD' to avoid saying his name. The meaning of this name is more important than its pronunciation and is derived from the context of the burning bush incident.

The Dutch theologian Herman Bavinck comments, 'The One who appears to Moses is not a new or strange God, but is the God of the fathers, the Unchangeable, the Immutable One who never leaves or forsakes his people but ever seeks his own and ever saves them, who is unchangeable in his grace, his love, in his succour, who will be what he is, since he ever remaineth himself.'[9] Bentley also explains God's Name against the background of the situation of his people. God 'was saying that he has personality – he is real and he is alive and active. He was also telling Moses that he had always existed. He was the God of Moses; he was Moses' God; and he would be the God of all the children of Abraham ... The God who always exists, always cares for his people.'[10] Therefore, God saw the affliction of his people and came to rescue them through his servant Moses.

We may wrongly imply from Exodus 6:2-3 that God was not known as 'LORD' before he spoke to Moses at the burning bush: 'I am the LORD. I appeared to Abraham, to Isaac and to Jacob as God Almighty, but by my name the LORD I did not make myself known to them.' Moses' mother's name, Jochebed, which means 'Jehovah is glory', reveals that God was already known as Jehovah. This verse must mean that the Lord now for the first time made known to Moses the *meaning* of his name. 'God Almighty' – El-Shaddai – means 'the Lord who is on high and sees everything' (see for example, Gen. 17:1). The name 'LORD' is a more personal name than 'El-Shaddai' and 'reflected a God who fulfils his promises. The promise of a coming exodus and redemption from slavery was not fulfilled during the time of the patriarchs but belonged to the distant future. The fact that the name Yahweh [LORD/

Jehovah/I AM] was made known to the Hebrews in the time of Moses meant that the fulfilment was now imminent.'[11]

The name 'I AM WHO I AM' also highlights the uniqueness of God; he *alone* is God. The Hebrews lived for over 400 years in Egypt, a land with many gods; therefore it was necessary for God to assert his uniqueness. He was not one god among many or the tribal god of the Jews, but the only true God who demanded exclusive worship and obedience. It is tragic how soon the people forgot this point and bowed down to a golden calf (Exod. 32).

Furthermore, God's name – Jehovah – couples with his other names to reveal different facets of his character, for example, the LORD who provides (Gen. 22:14); who heals (Exod. 15:22-26); our banner (Exod. 17:15); who makes us holy (Lev. 20:8); of peace (Judg. 6:24); our shepherd (Ps. 23); our judge (Ps.7:8; 96:13) and our righteousness (Jer. 23:5-6; 33:16). He is also 'The LORD Almighty' (Psalm 46:7 – 'The LORD of hosts' i.e. angels, AV/NKJV).

The Hebrew 'LORD' is translated as '*kurios*' in the Greek translation of the Old Testament (known as the Septuagint) and is used of Jesus Christ in the Greek New Testament. Writing to the Romans, Paul says 'Everyone who calls on the name of the Lord [*kurios*] will be saved' (Rom. 10:13, quoting Joel 2:32). Who is the 'Lord'? Verse 9 answers the question, 'If you confess with your mouth, "Jesus is Lord," [*kurios*] and believe in your heart that God raised him from the dead, you will be saved.' Jesus is the Lord! He is God the Son who came to earth to reveal God the Father.

'Before Abraham'

Jesus bases an argument on the present tense in the 'I AM WHO I AM' name of God when debating with the Sadducees who did not believe in the resurrection of the dead. 'But about the resurrection of the dead – have you not read what God said to you, "I am the God of Abraham, the God of Isaac, and the

God of Jacob"? He is not the God of the dead but of the living'
(Matt. 22:31-32). The present tense proves the point!

In another debate with the Jews, Jesus declared 'before
Abraham was born, I am!' His hearers knew that he was
referring to Exodus 3:14 and claiming equality with Jehovah,
therefore 'they picked up stones to stone him' (John 8:58-
59). 'Jesus is not only saying that he existed before Abraham,
but that he is the divine Son, one in essence with the great
"I AM" ... Jesus transcended time, for he was God! ... They
understood clearly that he was claiming to be the *divine* Son
of God. The mob deemed that to be blasphemous, and in
their outrage attempted to take the law of God into their own
hands (cf. Lev. 24:16).'[12] They failed, for 'Jesus hid himself,
slipping away from the temple grounds' (John 8:59).

How did Abraham rejoice at the thought of seeing
Christ's day (John. 8:56)? He grasped that God's promise –
'All peoples on earth will be blessed through you' (Gen. 12:3)
– would find its fulfilment in the coming of Messiah, the
Saviour of the world. Jesus, was in effect saying to the Jews, 'I
am the Messiah who Abraham looked for; you must accept
me as Messiah or reject the God of Abraham!'

Jesus' words in John 8:58 – 'Before Abraham was born,
I am' – affirm the statement of John 1:1-2: 'In the beginning
was the Word, and the Word was with God, and the Word
was God. He was with God in the beginning.' The eternal
Word – the Lord Jesus Christ – came to earth, not this time
in a theophany, but in a human body with a human nature,
'The Word became flesh and dwelt among us, and we beheld
His glory, the glory as of the only begotten of the Father, full
of grace and truth' (John 1:14, NKJV).

The New Testament writers emphasize the deity and
immutability of Christ in various places. For example, 'In the
past God spoke to our forefathers through the prophets at
many times and in various ways, but in these last days he
has spoken to us by his Son, whom he appointed heir of all
things, and through whom he made the universe. The Son is

the radiance of God's glory and the exact representation of his being, sustaining all things by his powerful word. After he had provided purification for sins, he sat down at the right hand of the Majesty in heaven ... about the Son he says, "Your throne, O God, will last for ever and ever, and righteousness will be the sceptre of your kingdom" ... He also says, "In the beginning, O Lord, you laid the foundations of the earth, and the heavens are the work of your hands. They will perish, but you remain; they will all wear out like a garment. You will roll them up like a robe; like a garment they will be changed. But you remain the same, and your years will never end'" (Heb. 1:1-3,8,10-12, quoting Ps. 45:6-7 and Ps. 102:25-27).

'I AM'

Jesus uses seven metaphors to describe his character; each one begins with the words 'I am', thus echoing Exodus 3:14, 'I AM WHO I AM'. The use of these titles 'by our Lord Jesus Christ at once identifies him as Jehovah of the Old Testament and confirms his deity.'[13] The 'I am sayings' are all found in the Gospel of John:

1. 'I am the bread of life' (6:35). 'As bread is the staple of daily life, so Christ is the staple of eternal life.'[14]
2. 'I am the light of the world' (8:12). 'Christ dispels the darkness whether of ignorance, wickedness, misery, alienation from God and man, or condemnation and a lost eternity in hell.'[15]
3. 'I am the door' (10:7,9, NKJV). He is the one and only door into the sheepfold – the church – and the one and only door into heaven.
4. 'I am the good shepherd' (10:11,14). The shepherd proves that he is 'excellent' (meaning of 'good') by dying on the cross for his sheep – he dies for them alone.
5. 'I am the resurrection and the life' (11:25). New life begins with Christ – eternal life as a gift to us now.

More than that, because he rose from the dead, we are guaranteed that when he returns we will be given new bodies to fit us for heaven.

6. 'I am the way and the truth and the life' (14:6). Christ 'is the way to salvation, to glory and to his Father's house'. He is the truth 'because he is God revealed to us'.[16] He is the life who gives us eternal life. He is the only way, truth and life.

7. 'I am the true vine' (15:1,5). Spiritual life comes from, and grows through, union with Jesus Christ.

Jesus is a glorious Saviour – we ought to do all we can to spread his fame!

Moses speaks to the Israelites

Moses told Aaron and then the Hebrew elders that God was going to rescue them from slavery and that he (Moses) was God's chosen deliverer. Their initial response is encouraging, 'They believed. And when they heard that the LORD was concerned about them and had seen their misery, they bowed down and worshipped' (Exod. 4:29-31). However, their attitude soon changes after Pharaoh demands that they provide their own straw for making bricks and commands the foreman to make the slaves work harder. 'You have made us a stench to Pharaoh and his officials and have put a sword in his hand to kill us' they complain (Exod. 5:21). God re-appears to Moses to reassure his servant that his purpose is to deliver his people and to give them the land promised to Abraham. What is the Hebrews' response? 'They did not listen to him because of their discouragement and cruel bondage' (Exod. 6:9).

4.
Christ the Messiah
—— (Exod. 3-11) ——

Moses' hesitant obedience contrasts with Christ's willing obedience expressed in Psalm 40:6-8 and commented on in Heb. 10:5-12 and Phil. 2:8-9. The signs (miracles) done through Moses are compared to the miracles of Christ. Both the miracles of Moses and Christ authenticate their ministries. Christ's miracles also demonstrate his deity. Pharaoh, like some of Christ's hearers, saw miracles but hardened his heart and even Jesus' own disciples, having witnessed miracles, were slow to believe. Who hardened Pharaoh's heart – Pharaoh or God? Both! We look at 'the hardening of the heart' in the light of Rom. 9:18. References to Israel, God's firstborn, are linked to Col. 1:18 and Heb. 12:23 where we read of Christ, 'the firstborn from the dead' and 'the church of the firstborn'.

'So now, go. I am sending you to Pharaoh to bring my people the Israelites out of Egypt', commands Christ from the burning bush (Exod. 3:10). Moses responds to this command by asking a question, 'Who am I, that I should go to Pharaoh?' (verse 11). Was Moses expressing his humility because he felt unworthy to represent God before Pharaoh? The narrative of Exodus 3-4 does not seem to support this view; rather these chapters suggest that Moses' words reveal his lack of confidence in God. Moses' five objections

(3:11,13; 4:1,10,13) provoke God to become angry with him (4:14). There is a limit even to the patience of God.

Eventually Moses obeys God's command by returning to Egypt and calling together the Israelite elders to tell them about God's promise to rescue his people from the misery of captivity and to lead them into 'a land flowing with milk and honey' (3:16-18; 4:18-31). Then Moses delivered God's message to Pharaoh: 'This is what the LORD, the God of Israel, says: "Let my people go"' (5:1). In the later chapters of Exodus which contain God's instructions concerning the tabernacle, we read that Moses did 'as the LORD commanded him' (40:19). Obeying God became the hallmark of Moses' life.

Obedience

Moses' hesitant obedience at the burning bush contrasts with the willing obedience of the Lord Jesus Christ, of whom Moses is a type. In the words of a Messianic Psalm, Christ says to his Father, 'I desire to do your will, O my God; your law is within my heart' (Ps. 40:8). The writer to the Hebrews identifies the speaker in this psalm as Christ (Heb. 10:5-12). Messiah's obedience led to the cross where he 'offered for all time one sacrifice for sins'. Paul makes a similar point when he writes to the Philippians: 'he humbled himself and became obedient to death – even death on a cross!' God rewarded the obedience of his Son by exalting him to the 'highest place'; he is now enthroned at 'the right hand of God' (Phil. 2:8-9). Followers of the obedient Messiah pray like Paul, 'Lord, what do You want me to do?' (Acts 9:6, NKJV).

Signs

Coming back to Exodus 3, we read that God encouraged fearful Moses by giving him a promise and a sign: 'I will be with you. And this will be the sign to you that it is I who have sent you: When you have brought the people out of Egypt, you will worship God on this mountain' (verse 12). All the events of Exodus 4 through to chapter 18 take place before Moses sees this 'sign' when he returns to Mount Sinai (Exod. 19). At Sinai, Moses and the Israelites see a display of the awesome presence of God. 'The sign is not given until Moses steps out in faith to go to Egypt and to do what God has commanded.' [1]

God also gave Moses three immediate signs to cure his doubts and to authenticate his commission. When Moses threw his staff on the ground, it became a snake and when he took the snake by the tail, it turned again into a staff. Furthermore, when Moses put his hand inside his cloak it became leprous. Healing came when he placed his hand back inside the cloak. If these two miracles did not convince the Israelites, then he was to take water from the Nile and pour it on dry ground. As he poured the water, it would become blood (Exod. 4:1-10). What happened when Moses performed these miracles in front of the elders of Israel? 'They believed. And when they heard that the LORD was concerned about them and had seen their misery, they bowed down and worshipped' (4:29-31).

Moses is the first person in the Old Testament to perform miracles; Jesus is the first person in the New Testament to perform miracles. What was the purpose of Jesus' miracles? To prove that he was the promised Messiah and the Son of God. Towards the end of his gospel, the apostle John wrote, 'Jesus did many other miraculous signs in the presence of his disciples, which are not recorded in this book. But these are written that you may believe that Jesus is the Christ, the Son of God, and that by believing you may have life in his name' (John 20:30-31). Following Jesus' first miracle, turning water into wine, we read that 'his disciples put their faith in him' because they saw in this miracle a revelation of God's glory. Shortly afterwards, we read that 'many people saw the miraculous signs he was doing and believed in his name' (John 2:11,23). However, it is important to remember that seeing miracles does not necessarily bring salvation. The

Pharisees, like Pharaoh, saw miracles but hardened their hearts (Exod. 8:15,32; 9:34; cf. Luke 16:31).

John the Baptist, who was imprisoned because he denounced Herod – the Roman official in Jerusalem – for his adultery, sends Jesus a question, asking if he is the promised Messiah. Doubts troubled even this courageous servant of God. 'Tell John', Jesus replies, 'that the blind see, the lame walk, the lepers are cleansed, the deaf hear, the dead are raised, the poor have the gospel preached to them' (Luke 7:22, NKJV). Why does Jesus point to his miracles as evidence that he is the Messiah? He is saying to John, 'Remember the words of Isaiah.' Some seven-hundred years before Jesus, Isaiah prophesied that the Messiah would open the eyes of the blind, the ears of the deaf and the mouths of the dumb; he would make the lame walk; he would preach the gospel to the poor (Isa. 35:4-6; 61:1-2).

Hard hearts

We have observed earlier in this chapter, that the Israelite elders saw Moses' signs and worshipped God (4:29-31). But how does Pharaoh react when he sees Moses' rod turn into a snake? He 'became hard and he would not listen to them, just as the LORD had said' (7:13; cf. 4:21). Does he have a change of heart when he sees blood, instead of water, in the Egyptian rivers or when he sees frogs in the palace? Not at all. We read 'Pharaoh's heart became hard' and again, 'he hardened his heart' (7:22; 8:15). Will a plague of gnats humble him? Not at all, even though his magicians declare, 'This is the finger of God' (8:19). Pharaoh continues to harden his heart after a plague of flies and a plague on his livestock. He remains unrepentant despite further plagues of hail, locusts and darkness (8:32; 9:7,34; 10:27). Though the death of Pharaoh's firstborn son compels him to release the Israelites, his armies soon pursue them to the Red Sea (Exod. 11-12).

'Who is the LORD, that I should obey him and let Israel go?' sneers the proud Pharaoh (5:2). The plagues (Exod. 7-11) are

God's answer to this question; they demonstrate that God is more powerful than the mightiest men and more importantly, he is greater than all the gods of Egypt. The plagues on Israel also anticipate the dreadful day of judgement (Rev. 20:11-15). Who is the Judge? Richard Brooks answers this question, 'It is God himself who is seated on the throne, but he judges the world through his Son, the Lord Jesus Christ. In this matter, as ever, the Father and the Son are one (John 10:30). But it serves to remind us that the Father has committed authority and judgement to the Son (Matt. 28:18; John 5:22-27) and that how we fare on the judgement day will depend upon our relationship to Christ himself.' [2]

Pharaoh will not believe no matter how much evidence of God's power he sees with his own eyes. Likewise, many heard Jesus, God the Son, and saw his miracles but would not believe. Shortly before his death, Jesus laments for the nation – 'Jerusalem' represents Israel – that had rejected him, 'O Jerusalem, Jerusalem, you who kill the prophets and stone those sent to you, how often I have longed to gather your children together, as a hen gathers her chicks under her wings, but you were not willing' (Matt. 23:37). Christ came to change hard hearts into soft, tender hearts that beat with love for him – this he does through the Holy Spirit's work of regeneration (Ezek. 36:25-27).

Sadly, even Jesus' own disciples were so slow to believe that Jesus speaks of the hardness of their hearts. When the terrified disciples saw Jesus walking on water and calming the storm on the Sea of Galilee, Mark comments that 'their hearts were hardened.' On another occasion, when 'the disciples had forgotten to bring bread, except for one loaf … Jesus asked them "Why are you talking about having no bread? Do you still not see or understand? Are your hearts hardened? Do you have eyes but fail to see, and ears but fail to hear?"' Jesus reminded his disciples of the twelve baskets and seven baskets of pieces of bread and fish left after he miraculously fed the five thousand and four thousand (Mark 6:30-52, especially note verse 52; 8:1-21, especially note verse 17). What was the difference between the Jew's hardness and that of the disciples? The Jews, especially the leaders such as the Pharisees, were obstinate in their unbelief, whereas the disciples were true believers but slow to grasp spiritual truth.

The writer to the Hebrews, citing Psalm 95:7-8, appeals to Christians on the verge of backsliding, 'do not harden your hearts' (Heb. 3:7-11; 4:7). We harden our hearts when we do not pay attention to what we have heard so that we drift away from our Christian faith. The cure for backsliding is to 'fix our eyes on Jesus' by considering what he suffered to save us from sin (Heb. 2:1-3; 12:1-4). David's words in Psalm 95 look back to the constant unbelief and disobedience of the Israelites in the wilderness (see for example Exodus 16-17). The generation that left Egypt at the Exodus did not enter into the promised land of Canaan.

God's sovereignty

Why do some, like the Israelite elders, believe and worship (Exod. 4:29-31) while others, like Pharaoh, reject God? The answer lies in God's sovereignty. A refrain that runs through Exodus chapters 4-14 is 'The LORD hardened Pharaoh's heart' (Exod. 4:21; 7:3; 9:12; 10:1,20,27; 11:10; 14:4,8,17). Pharaoh freely chose to defy God, nevertheless, to use Currid's words, 'God is the cause of that hardening.' [3] He later explains, 'It is clear that God does not make Pharaoh evil … What God simply does is harden Pharaoh in his nature by giving him completely over to his sin (Rom. 1:24-26). Is this unfair of God? Absolutely not. As Paul comments, God "has mercy on whom he desires, and he hardens whom he desires" (Rom. 9:18). Moreover, Pharaoh is responsible for his condition. It is not as if God is hardening a good person. Frankly, Pharaoh has no claim upon God's mercy, for he has sinned wilfully and maliciously. He is no innocent bystander, but a willing, desiring compatriot of sin and vileness.' [4] Bentley comments

'Those who deliberately turn aside from God's way discover that God himself will turn against them in judgement.'[5]

We see this interplay between divine sovereignty and human responsibility in the execution of Christ. Treacherous Judas, scheming religious leaders and wicked Roman officials acted freely, but unwittingly fulfilled the decrees of the sovereign God. Listen to Peter preaching on the day of Pentecost, facing the murderers of Jesus: 'This man was handed over to you by God's set purpose and foreknowledge; and you, with the help of wicked men, put him to death by nailing him to the cross' (Acts 2:23). Following the miraculous healing of a lame man, the Jewish Council, known as the Sanhedrin, arrest John and Peter. On their release, they join the believers in Jerusalem for prayer in which they praise God for his sovereignty: 'Herod and Pontius Pilate met together with the Gentiles and the people of Israel in this city to conspire against your holy servant Jesus, whom you anointed. They did what your power and will had decided beforehand should happen' (Acts 4:27-28). Peter takes up this theme again in his first letter: 'You were redeemed ... with the precious blood of Christ, a lamb without blemish or defect. He was chosen before the creation of the world, but was revealed in these last times for your sake' (1 Peter 1:18-20). Christ's death was no divine after-thought when Adam sinned; God had already planned redemption before creation. Moreover, God chose the redeemed before creation (see 1 Peter 1:1-2). A realisation of God's electing love should not lead to pride but to praise.

The firstborn

Why do the plagues reach their climax with the death of the firstborn Egyptian sons, including Pharaoh's own son? God himself explains the reason to Moses and commands him to tell Pharaoh: 'Israel is my firstborn son, and I told you, "Let my son go, so he may worship me." But you refused to let him go; so I will kill your firstborn' (Exod. 4:22-23). Egyptians and Hebrews treated the firstborn as a position of prominence and pre-eminence. Christ is God's firstborn, now enthroned in heaven, the first of many sons to be raised from the dead. His sons are known as 'the church of the firstborn' (Col. 1:15-20; Heb. 12:18-24).

5.

Christ the Passover Lamb

————————— (Exod. 12) —————————

Exodus 12 highlights the seriousness of sin, God's way of redemption and the need of faith. God spared Israel, his firstborn, because he saw the lamb's blood spread on the doorframes. God spares the sinner who trusts in Christ our Passover Lamb (1 Cor. 5:7). Six parallels are suggested between the Passover lamb and Christ our Lamb. Exodus 12 links to Hebrews 11:28, where we read of the faith of Moses who believed God's instructions for the Passover night and God's promises of deliverance from Egypt. The final section of this chapter comments on the feast of unleavened bread (Exod. 12:14-20) in the light of Paul's teaching in 1 Corinthians 5:6-8.

There are several New Testament keys to unlock Exodus 12, for example, 'Get rid of the old yeast that you may be a new batch without yeast – as you really are. For Christ, our Passover lamb has been sacrificed' (1 Cor. 5:7). Another key is 'By faith he [Moses] kept the Passover and the sprinkling of blood, so that the destroyer of the firstborn would not touch the firstborn of Israel' (Heb. 11:28).

We read in Exodus 12 about the Passover (verses 1-13,21-30) eaten on the 'fourteenth day of the month' (verse 6) and the seven-day feast of Unleavened Bread (verses 14-20) celebrated between the fifteenth and twenty-first days of the month Abib (known as Nisan after the exile).

God warned Pharaoh, through Moses, that if he refused to release his firstborn son Israel from slavery, then he would kill the proud monarch's firstborn son (Exod. 4:21-23). God fulfilled this threat when Pharaoh refused to free God's people despite having seen God's awesome power in nine plagues (Exod. 7-10).

Obeying God's instructions, each Jewish family killed a lamb and spread its blood on the doorposts of their houses. When the angel of death passed over Israel, he spared the firstborn sons in the blood-protected households but killed the Egyptian firstborn sons, including Pharaoh's, in the homes without the symbolic blood on the door lintels. What then is the spiritual significance of this dramatic event? What does it teach us about Christ the Passover Lamb?

1. The Passover (12:1-13)

The Passover ritual highlights ...

The seriousness of sin

The sprinkled blood on the doorposts protected the firstborn Israelite sons from death. Why did God threaten his own covenant people? Because they were sinners! Their bitterness towards Moses, their deliverer, proves the point (Exod. 5:21; 6:9). Further proof comes from the lips of Joshua, Moses' successor, who urged the people to 'throw away the gods your forefathers worshipped ... in Egypt, and serve the Lord' (Josh. 24:14-15). The Hebrews were as much sinners as Pharaoh and the Egyptians. We too are sinners! (Rom. 3:23).

God's way of redemption

A lamb dies; the firstborn lives. Christ our Passover Lamb dies; we live. The lamb dies in the place of the sinner: 'When I see the blood, I will pass over you' (Exod. 12:13). This is God's way of redemption then and now. God's way is 'no blood shed; no pardon of sin' (Heb. 9:22). God gave the Jews detailed instructions about the Passover lamb, which they neglected at their peril.

The lamb was killed by God's command. 'The LORD said to Moses … take a lamb … slaughter [it] at twilight' (Exod. 12:1,3,6). Christ also died because of God's command: 'The reason my Father loves me is that I lay down my life – only to take it up again. No-one takes it from me, but I lay it down of my own accord. I have authority to lay it down and authority to take it up again. This command I received from my Father' (John 10:17-18). God, who planned the Passover lamb's death, planned Christ's death. Peter facing the murderers of the Lord Jesus declared, 'This man was handed over to you by God's set purpose and foreknowledge; and you, with the help of wicked men, put him to death by nailing him to the cross' (Acts 2:23). Those who disobeyed God's command mourned the loss of their firstborn sons; those who reject Christ, God's Lamb, suffer eternal death.

The lamb was perfect. 'The animals you choose must be year-old males without defect, and you may take them from the sheep or the goats' (Exod. 12:5). The holy God demanded an unblemished sacrifice. Years later the apostle Peter wrote, 'You were redeemed … with the precious blood of Christ, a lamb without blemish or defect' (1 Peter 1:18,19). Christ's sinlessness is emphasised in many other passages of Scripture. For example, Gabriel tells the virgin mother, 'the holy one to be born will be called the Son of God.' Paul and the writer to the Hebrews agree with Peter: 'God made him who had no sin to be sin for us'; 'such a high priest meets our need – one who is holy, blameless, pure, set apart from sinners, exalted above the heavens' (Luke 1:35; 2 Cor. 5:21; Heb. 7:26). Christ the sinless Lamb achieved what the Passover lamb and no other sacrificial animals could ever accomplish – the pardon of sins (Heb. 10:3-4,11-12). Only a sinless Lamb could atone for sin.

The lamb's blood was sprinkled on the doorposts for protection. 'When the LORD goes through the land to strike down the Egyptians, he will see the blood on the top and sides of the doorframe and will pass over that doorway, and he will not permit the destroyer to enter your houses and strike you down' (Exod. 12:23, see also verses 7,12,13,22). A dead lamb or goat would not give protection; only sprinkled blood saved the firstborn son's life. Turning again to Peter we read about 'obedience to Jesus Christ and sprinkling by his blood' and the writer to the Hebrews exhorts us to 'draw near to God with a sincere heart in full assurance of faith, having our hearts sprinkled to cleanse us from a guilty conscience and having our bodies washed with pure water' (1 Peter 1:2; Heb. 10:22). The blood of Christ must be applied to the believer's heart and conscience. When we come in faith to God through Christ, his blood removes sin's stain from the soul and washes sin's guilt from the conscience. Once washed we may boldly approach the throne of the holy God! Once washed we are safe from God's wrath! Once washed we look forward to an eternity in the presence of God!

The lamb was eaten. 'That same night they are to eat the meat' (Exod. 12:8). Following his miraculous feeding of the five thousand, Jesus said, 'I tell you the truth, unless you eat the flesh of the Son of Man and drink his blood, you have no life in you' (John 6:53). What does Jesus mean? He is explaining how we become Christians. Just as food and drink, when eaten, become part of us, so we feed by faith on Christ to receive and to sustain spiritual life (verse 57). How do we feed on Christ? As we feed on his Word. 'The words I have spoken to you are spirit and they are life' (verse 63). Christ becomes 'the believer's never-ending banquet. He feasts on Christ now. He will feast on Christ forever.'[1]

The lamb was 'roasted over the fire' (Exod. 12:8). The death of Christ, the Passover Lamb, was 'a fragrant offering and sacrifice to God' (Eph. 5:2). God was pleased with the display of Christ's love in willingly dying for us on the cross. Another passage in which Paul writes about fragrance is 2 Corinthians 2:14-16 where we read: 'But thanks be to God, who always leads us in triumphal procession in Christ and through us spreads everywhere the fragrance of the knowledge of him. For we are to God the aroma of Christ among those who are being saved and those who are perishing. To the one we are the smell of death; to the other, the fragrance of life. And who is equal to such a task?' Our service is a delightful aroma to God and 'the fragrance of life' to believers but is 'the smell of death' to unbelievers. Some believe and receive eternal life; others reject the gospel and later receive eternal death.

The lamb was eaten with 'bread made without yeast' (Exod. 12:8). Yeast is a biblical symbol of evil (Matt. 16:5-12; Mark 8:14-15; Luke 12:1-2; 1 Cor. 5:6-8; Gal. 5:9). To benefit from Christ's death we must repent of sin and aim to live a holy life.

The lamb's bones were not broken. God's command is 'Do not break any of the bones' (Exod. 12:46). David wrote of the righteous man in Psalm 34:20, 'he [God] protects all his bones, not one of them will be broken.' John sees this verse as a prediction of Christ's unbroken bones when he died on the cross: 'These things happened so that the scripture would be fulfilled: "Not one of his bones will be broken"' (John 19:36). Breaking the bones of the crucified hastened death. It was after Christ had triumphantly cried, 'It is finished' and 'bowed his head and gave up his spirit' (John 19:30), that a soldier 'pierced Jesus' side with a spear, bringing a sudden flow of blood and water' (verse 34). The blood and water may suggest that the spear ruptured the heart of the Saviour. However, John's reason for mentioning this fact is not to describe what caused Jesus' death but to show that he was really dead. He also sees Jesus' piercing as a fulfilment of Zechariah 12:10, 'They will look on the one they have pierced' (verse 37). The apostle John quotes Zechariah again in Revelation 1:7, 'Look, he is coming with the clouds, and every eye will see him, even those who pierced him; and all the peoples of the earth will mourn because of him. So shall it be! Amen.' Sinners will mourn in remorse rather than repentance. When Christ comes it will be too late to seek his mercy because 'Now is the time of God's favour, now is the day of salvation' (2 Cor. 6:2). When Jesus was speaking of his return, he also quoted Zechariah's prophecy (Matt. 24:30).

The 19th century commentators, Jamieson, Faussett and Brown, see in Christ's unbroken bones 'a remarkable divine interposition to protect the sacred body of Christ from the last indignity after He had finished the work given Him to do. Every imaginable indignity had been permitted before that, up to the moment of His death. But no sooner is that over than an Unseen Hand is found to have provided against the clubs of the rude soldiers coming in contact with that temple of the Godhead.' [2]

The necessity of faith

We read in Hebrews 11:28: 'By faith he [Moses] kept the Passover and the sprinkling of blood, so that the destroyer of the firstborn would not touch the firstborn of Israel.' What is faith? It is to believe what God has said so that we act on his Word. God told Moses and the Israelites to kill a lamb and to sprinkle its blood on the doorframes. Did they have faith so that they acted on God's Word? Yes – 'The Israelites did just what the LORD commanded Moses and Aaron' (Exod. 12:28).

2. The Feast of Unleavened Bread (12:14-20)

God commanded his people, through Moses, to 'remove the yeast from your houses' – the penalty for disobedience was to 'be cut off from Israel' (verse 15). This is not a reference to a violent or premature death, or even to eternal death, but rather means that the offender lost 'the covenant rights and privileges normally afforded an Israelite.[3] The disobedient Hebrew was treated as a non-Jew, no longer one of God's chosen people and therefore no better than a pagan.

The apostle Paul applies this practice to Christians in 1 Corinthians 5:6-8: 'Your boasting is not good. Don't you know that a little yeast works through the whole batch of dough? Get rid of the old yeast that you may be a new batch without yeast – as you really are. For Christ, our Passover lamb, has been sacrificed. Therefore let us keep the Festival, not with the old yeast, the yeast of malice and wickedness, but with bread without yeast, the bread of sincerity and truth.' Immorality in the Corinthian church forms the backdrop for the apostle's words (verses 1-2). The Corinthians boasted about their profound knowledge and their remarkable gifts but they had failed to learn the basic lesson that unconfessed sin and undisciplined members affect the whole church. Bad example contradicts and undermines biblical preaching.

Paul gives two reasons for dealing with sin. Firstly, God has changed our lives. 'You really are', even now, 'a new batch without yeast' (verse 7). God has removed the yeast of sin from our lives; however, some sin remains and must be decisively removed. To express the matter theologically: God removing the yeast is regeneration or the new birth, whereas getting rid of 'the old yeast' is the ongoing work of holiness through the power of the Holy Spirit.

The second reason for dealing with sin is that Christ, our Passover, died to deliver us from sin. Christ's suffering on the cross is a powerful motive for us to deal with individual and corporate sin. We ought to be firm with ourselves – 'For if you live according to the sinful nature, you will die; but if by the Spirit you put to death the misdeeds of the body, you will live' (Rom. 8:13) – but gentle with others – 'Brothers, if someone is caught in a sin, you who are spiritual should restore him gently. But watch yourself, or you also may be tempted' (Gal. 6:1).

What then does Paul mean when he tells us to 'keep the Festival'? (1 Cor. 5:8). The rest of the verse makes it clear that he is not talking about the Passover or the Lord's Supper; to 'keep the Festival' is to replace sinful conduct ('malice and wickedness') with godly behaviour ('sincerity and truth'). Charles Hodge was right when he paraphrased Paul as saying, 'Let your whole lives be as a sacred festival.'[4] The Passover was eaten on one day and the Feast of Unleavened Bread ran for seven days but the festival of holiness is a lifelong celebration. Spiritual worship is offering our bodies as living sacrifices to God (Rom. 12:1-2).

6.

Christ the Saviour

—— **(Exod. 14)** ——

The Israelites hear the pursuing Egyptians behind them and see the Red Sea in front of them. God saves his people from destruction by opening a path through the Red Sea. This is a picture of God delivering us from Satan, a greater enemy than Pharaoh. Christ defeated Satan at Calvary. Exod. 14 links to Heb. 11:29 and the faith of Moses and the Israelites in crossing the Red Sea and also to 1 Cor. 10:1-3 where Paul writes about Israel 'baptised into Moses'. These words are explained in the context of 1 Cor. 10 that looks back to events in the book of Exodus. After comments on Moses' song after the Red Sea crossing in Exod. 15, we consider the grumbling of the people at the end of chapter. What a sad response to such an amazing deliverance!

Picture the scene: behind the escaped Hebrews is the pursuing army of Pharaoh riding in 'six hundred of the best chariots, along with all the other chariots of Egypt'; in front of them is the Red Sea. There is no escape route – or so it seems to the terrified Israelites who chide Moses because he led them from slavery to freedom. 'It would have been better for us to serve the Egyptians than to die in the desert!' they scream at Moses (Exod. 14:10-12). Grumbling at Moses, God's appointed leader, and hankering after Egypt became a pattern for the nomad Israelites. What does Moses do? He calmly declares 'Do not be afraid. Stand firm and you will see the deliverance the LORD will bring you today. The Egyptians you see today you will never see again. The LORD will fight for you; you need only to be still' (verses 13-14). Then God tells Moses to 'Raise your staff and stretch out your hand over the sea to divide the water so that the Israelites can go through on dry ground' (verses 15-16). It is at this point in the narrative that we read that 'the angel of God', the pre-incarnate Christ, 'who had been travelling in front of Israel's army, withdrew and went behind them. The pillar of cloud also moved from in front and stood behind them, coming between the armies of Egypt and Israel. Throughout the night the cloud brought darkness to the one side and light to the other; so neither went near the other all night' (verses 19-20). The rest of Exodus 14 relates the dramatic deliverance of the Israelites and the destruction of Pharaoh's army (verses 21-31).

The mighty Saviour

Exodus 14 is about Christ the mighty Saviour. The word 'deliverance' in verse 13 reads as 'salvation' in the AV/NKJV. After the Red Sea crossing, we read that 'The LORD saved Israel from the hands of the Egyptians' (verse 30). 'The LORD' is the 'I AM WHO I AM', Christ, who spoke to Moses at the burning bush (3:14).

The Hebrews could do nothing to deliver themselves from Pharaoh's army – destruction seemed inevitable. Neither can the sinner rescue himself from Satan, the enemy of souls, who is far more powerful than Pharaoh. Satan traps sinners and takes 'them captive to do his will'. He confuses their minds so that they cannot see God's glory in Christ. He fills their hearts with sinful cravings and drives them towards hell. He keeps his victims in a state of spiritual death. Apart from God's intervention eternal death is inescapable (2 Tim. 2:26; 2 Cor. 4:4; Eph. 2:1-3).

Satan is powerful, but Jesus Christ is almighty! Christ by his death tied up the devil, the strong man, and stole his possessions, enslaved unbelievers (Mark 3:27). In fact, the rescued captives belonged to Christ because God gave them to his Son before his incarnation. The real thief was Satan himself! (John 6:37; 17:6,9). Paul writes about Christ's defeat of Satan and demons in his letter to the Colossians. Christ 'disarmed the powers and authorities, he made a public spectacle of them, triumphing over them by the cross' (Col. 2:15). Christ is God, the creator of angels, and therefore above good and bad (fallen) angels (Col. 1:16-19; 2:9-10). The word 'disarmed' refers to a person stripping off his clothes; Christ stripped Satan and his demons of their enslaving power. The word 'triumphing' comes from the Roman emperors leading prisoners of war in procession before a cheering public. At Calvary, Christ defeated Satan and sealed his doom. True, Satan roars like a lion. However, he is a chained lion and cannot therefore rob God's elect of salvation. By God's power, we may resist the devil and see him run! (1 Peter 5:8-9; Jas. 4:7).

The evidence of Satan's defeat is the rescue of sinners from his kingdom. God 'has rescued us from the dominion of darkness and brought us into the kingdom of the Son he loves, in whom we have redemption, the forgiveness of sins' (Col. 1:13-14). Another result of Satan's defeat is that the redeemed in heaven, drawn from all the nations of the world, will be too many to count. The saints in heaven declare that Christ is the only Saviour: 'salvation belongs to our God, who sits on the throne, and to the Lamb' (Rev 7:10).

We see a foreshadowing of Christ's disarming of Satan in his defeat of the Egyptian Pharaoh. The overthrow of Pharaoh, and of Satan, brings glory to God. (Exod. 14:17-18; 23-28; 15:1-12,19-21). The defeat of Pharaoh, and of Satan, brings deliverance to God's people; they are 'the people you have redeemed' (15:13). Christ, who overthrew Pharaoh, will send Satan and his servants into 'the lake of burning sulphur … They will be tormented day and night for ever and ever' (Rev. 20:10).

'By faith'

God alone saved the Israelites from Pharaoh's army; nevertheless his people must follow Moses into the Red Sea. Crossing the Red Sea demanded faith. What is faith? Believing what God says so that we obey him. Moses believed God's Word: 'Raise your staff and stretch out your hand over the sea to divide the water so that the Israelites can go through on dry ground.' The Israelites believed God's Word through Moses so that they 'went through the sea on dry ground, with a wall of water on their right and on their left' (Exod. 14:15-16, 21-22). The writer to the Hebrews commends the Israelites' faith: 'By faith the people passed through the Red Sea as on dry land; but when the Egyptians tried to do so, they were drowned' (Heb. 11:29).

Imagine you are standing by the Red Sea with the Egyptians in hot pursuit! 'Would you not think twice before walking on the sea bed with a wall of water towering above you on either side? Could you be certain that the whole mass of it would not come crashing down? Was God playing with them? The only way of escape was to walk right through the jaws of a watery death. They had to believe that God would do as he had said. His power was terrifying. Could they be sure of it? Would he use that awesome power to crush them or save them?'[1]

Christ alone saves from Satan's clutches; however, the sinner must go to him in faith. Christ says that he will never drive away anyone who comes to him for pardon (John 6:37) – do you believe his promise? God says in his Word that 'Christ Jesus came into the world to save sinners' (1 Tim. 1:15) – do you believe him?

God saves the believing Israelites and destroys the unbelieving Egyptians. 'This incident happened over 3,000 years ago, but it leaves us with something to ponder. According to the Bible, that same power will have a role to play in every human life. Ultimately, a similar fate lies in store for us all. Either God will save us, or he will destroy us ... eternal security or eternal ruin ... Some respond to Jesus' invitation, others do not. It is faith that distinguishes them. Do you have faith? It involves more than words. It begins with a decisive choice. It commits itself to a life of steady endurance ... You do not need a mighty faith to win through, but faith in a mighty God.'[2]

Jude's warning

Jude comments on God's deliverance of his people and the destruction of the Egyptians in the Red Sea: 'The Lord delivered his people out of Egypt, but later destroyed those who did not believe' (verse 5). Some old Greek manuscripts have 'Jesus' rather than 'Lord' and this reading is used in the English Standard Version.

Jude warns his readers about the doom of ungodly people masquerading as Christians. On Judgement Day Christ will separate the sheep (true believers) from the goats (unbelievers) (Matt. 25:31-46). To an untrained eye, from a distance, goats sometimes look like sheep but the shepherd knows the difference! Christ who delivered his people and destroyed the Egyptians, has perfect wisdom; he is not deceived.

'Baptised into Moses'

The apostle Paul also comments on the Israelites crossing the Red Sea: 'For I do not want you to be ignorant of the fact, brothers, that our forefathers were all under the cloud and that they all passed through the sea. They were all baptised into Moses in the cloud and the sea' (1 Cor. 10:1-2). The word 'For' links these verses to 9:27 and Paul's concern that having 'preached to others, I myself will not be disqualified for the prize'. Can Christians lose their salvation? 'The danger is not of falling from salvation but of falling from holiness and from usefulness in service.'³ The 'brothers' are mostly non-Jewish believers, so why write to them about 'our forefathers' and events in Jewish history to enforce his teaching? Because those who have the faith of Abraham are his spiritual descendants (Rom. 2:28-29; 4:11; 9:6; Gal. 3:29).

How do these stories from ancient history relate to the Corinthians, and what is their message for us? 'Now these things occurred as examples to keep us from setting our hearts on evil things as they did. Do not be idolaters ... We should not commit sexual immorality ... We should not test the Lord ... And do not grumble ... So, if you think you are standing firm, be careful that you don't fall!' (1 Cor. 10:6-12).

What then does Paul mean when he says that the Israelites were 'baptised into Moses' (verse 2)? 'That cloud under which they walked out of Egypt and that sea through which they passed effectively separated them from their old life and identified them with a new leader, Moses, and a new life.'⁴ Believers are 'baptised into Christ' (Rom. 6:3; Gal 3:27). Baptism separates us from our old life. We 'live a new life ... our old self was crucified with him so that ... we should no longer be slaves to sin' (Rom. 6:4-7). Furthermore, 'Water baptism symbolises the baptism believers have already experienced. When we trust in Jesus Christ we are baptised into Him, identified with Him, made one with Him.'⁵

The pillar of cloud and fire

The reference to the 'cloud' in 1 Corinthians 10:1 refers to the 'pillar of cloud' mentioned in Exodus 13:21-22, several times throughout chapter 14, and frequently in subsequent chapters. Currid comments on chapter 13:21-22: 'Moses now presents Yahweh [Jehovah] in theophany ... Often he would appear as a glory cloud, called the Shekinah glory by some writers. The glory cloud was a visible symbol of God's presence among his people ... In the present story we see Yahweh in a double theophany ... so that Yahweh would be with his people and lead them "by day" and "by night". The use of the two opposites underscores the all-inclusive nature of God's presence with Israel ... Although they were traversing unknown territory they had no need to fear, Yahweh "was going before them", guiding, directing and leading them.'[6] Commenting on Exodus 14:19-20, Currid clearly identifies the pillar of cloud as 'the Shekinah glory by which God makes his presence known'.[7]

The Song of Moses

Imagine the spontaneous singing of over two million people praising God, led by Moses and his sister Miriam, accompanied by tambourines and the sound of the dancing feet of women. This is the first song recorded in the Bible and expresses the Israelites' relief after safely crossing the Red Sea. Moses' song centres on the 'Lord', (this name occurs thirteen times in Exodus 15:1-21) and divides into four sections: the Lord's triumph (verses 1-5), power (verses 6-10), uniqueness (verses 11-12) and protection (verses 13-17). Moses looks back to what God has done in verses 1-12 and then sings about what God will do in verses 14-18. Moses contrasts God's power with Pharaoh's pride (verses 7,9-10, 21). The grand finale of Moses' song is the affirmation of verse 18, 'The Lord will reign for ever and ever.'

In Revelation 15, the aged apostle John hears echoes of Moses' ancient song. He writes in verse 2-3 of God's people playing harps and singing 'the song of Moses ... and the song of the Lamb'. Why should the exiled John remind persecuted 1st century believers of Moses' song? The mighty Saviour who drowned Pharaoh's armies in the Red Sea will defend his tormented people and crush the Roman Empire. And why does John add the song of the Lamb to the song of Moses? Because the conquering Lord of the Exodus is the slain Lamb of Revelation. The Lamb's song will be sung eternally by thousands of angels and the 'great multitude' of the elect:

'Worthy is the Lamb, who was slain, to receive power and wealth and wisdom and strength and honour and glory and praise!' (Rev. 5:12; see also verse 13 and 7:9-11). Even now on earth, whatever our temptations and trials, we may sing this song of the Lamb!

Grumbling

Exodus 14 ends on a high note followed by the exuberant song of chapter 15: 'And when the Israelites saw the great power the LORD displayed against the Egyptians, the people feared the LORD and put their trust in him and in Moses his servant' (14:31). Nevertheless, turning to the end of chapter 15 and reading into chapter 17 we hear the Israelites grumbling yet again against God and his servant Moses. They lost sight of their gracious God and Saviour. Is your faith real or only temporary? We ought to heed Paul's exhortation, 'Examine yourselves to see whether you are in the faith; test yourselves. Do you not realise that Christ Jesus is in you – unless, of course, you fail the test?' (2 Cor. 13:5). True faith rests on Christ alone for salvation and results in godly living.

7.

Christ the True Bread

———— (Exod. 16) ————

*God graciously gives his grumbling people food.
He is our heavenly Father who cares for us (Matt. 6). He
provides food for the body and food for the soul. Exod. 16
links to John 6 where Jesus says 'I am the bread of life' and
compares himself to the manna in the wilderness. Those
who ate the manna died but those who eat Christ by faith
receive eternal life. We read about manna in two other NT
passages, Heb. 9:4 and Rev. 2:17.*

The travelling Jews enjoyed their rest at Elim, the place
of 'twelve springs' and 'seventy palm trees' (Exod.
15:27). All too soon, they heard God's command to move on
further into the hot, uninviting desert and before long food-
supplies ran short. Then the Israelites grumbled against their
deliverer Moses. Their mouths watered as they thought of
'the pots of meat' and 'all the food we wanted' back in Egypt;
they forgot the frequent beatings and the degrading slavery
and they exaggerated the occasional blessings. 'You have
brought us out into this desert to starve this entire assembly
to death' they complained to Moses (Exod. 16:3). Their
leader warned them: 'You are not grumbling against us, but
against the LORD'; they were in danger of punishment from
God (verse 8). Their talk of starvation seems rather extreme
when we recall that the Jews left Egypt, only three months

before, with 'large droves of livestock, both flocks and herds' (Exod. 12:38).

The 17th century Puritan William Gurnall comments: 'All Israel followed Moses joyfully out of Egypt. But when their stomachs were a little pinched with hunger they preferred the bondage of Pharaoh to the promised blessings of Israel. How many part with Christ at the crossroad of suffering!'[1]

Bread from heaven

God's response to the Israelites' grumbling came as a surprise: 'I will rain down bread from heaven' (Exod. 16:4). The Lord sent manna for every day, without fail, for forty years; it came as 'thin flakes like frost on the ground' and 'was white like coriander seed and tasted like wafers made with honey'. When the Jews first saw 'the bread from heaven' they could not identify this strange substance and therefore they called it 'manna', which simply means 'what is it?' (verses 14,31,35). God generously gave quails to eat with the bread (verse 13). The Lord answered murmuring with mercy.

Why did God give his undeserving people bread? He gave them manna to test 'whether they will follow my instructions' (verse 4). Some did exactly what God said; others disobeyed him and kept the manna overnight and discovered in the morning that it was 'full of maggots and began to smell' (verses 19-20). God gave his people two days' supply on Friday and commanded his people not to go looking for manna on the Sabbath. 'Nevertheless, some of the people went out on the seventh day to gather it, but they found none. Then the LORD said to Moses, "How long will you refuse to keep my commands and my instructions?"' (Verses 22-28). Many of the Israelites failed the test. The grumblers were disobedient, but even so, God gave them manna and quails! The gracious God 'does not treat us as our sins deserve or repay us according to our iniquities' (Ps. 103:10).

The second reason why God gave his people manna was that 'you will know that it was the LORD who brought you out of Egypt' (verses 6,11-12). Currid comments 'One of the major points of the entire text of Exodus is the recognition of Yahweh as God over all.'[2] Grumbling expressed rebellion against the God who is over all. We read in verse 10 that 'While Aaron was speaking to the whole Israelite community, they looked toward the desert, and there was the glory of the LORD appearing in the cloud' – the cloud that had been leading them in the wilderness (13:21-22; 14:19-24). 'The glory cloud was a visible symbol of God's presence among his people'[3] – a theophany – a pre-incarnate appearance of Christ. 'This extraordinary sign of the glory of God appeared in the desert, partly to show the estrangement of the murmuring nation from its God, but still more to show to the people, that God could glorify Himself by bestowing gifts upon His people even in the barren wilderness. For Jehovah spoke to Moses out of this sign, and confirmed to the people what Moses had promised them.'[4]

Our heavenly Father

What do we learn from Exodus 16? The God of heaven loves his people though they do not deserve his kindness. He is our heavenly Father who provides all our needs. The wilderness preservation is a remarkable illustration of Jesus' teaching in Matthew 6:25-30: 'Therefore I tell you, do not worry about your life, what you will eat or drink; or about your body, what you will wear. Is not life more important than food, and the body more important than clothes? Look at the birds of the air; they do not sow nor reap or store away in barns, and yet your heavenly Father feeds them. Are you not much more valuable than they? ... If that is how God clothes the grass of the field, which is here today and tomorrow is thrown into the fire, will he not much more clothe you, O you of little faith?' God, who miraculously fed over two million Jews every day for forty years in the inhospitable desert with manna and quails, can look after us in all the varied circumstances of our lives. The manna came one day at a time, except on the Sabbath (Saturday), so God provides what we need, though not always what we want, as the need arises. The Lord Jesus Christ our 'great high priest' promises from 'the throne of grace ... to help us in our time of need' (Heb. 4:16).

The hunger of the soul

However, there is a deeper hunger than that of the body; it is a hunger of the soul for God's pardon and presence. This is the hunger which compels us to 'seek first his kingdom and his righteousness' (Matt. 6:33). Jesus spoke about this hunger after he fed 5,000 people with five loaves and two fishes: 'I am the bread of life. He who comes to me will never go hungry, and he who believes in me will never be thirsty' (John 6:35). He is the true bread from heaven, manna for hungry souls (verses 32-33). So then, Jesus in John 6 gives us the key to unlock the spiritual significance of the manna in the wilderness.

Jesus' claim to be the bread of life was made just after the Jews had demanded a miracle greater than Moses' giving manna in the wilderness (verse 30). These Jews saw Jesus feed 5,000 people, but now insisted on something even more spectacular. Henry Mahan suggests 'They may have been saying, "You fed five thousand once, but in Moses' day our forefathers ate the bread for forty years. We are interested in continual prosperity."'[5] Sadly, they valued dramatic gifts more than the generous Giver. Jesus reminded his critics that the manna came from God, not Moses (verse 32) and then he urged them to hunger not for gifts but for himself (verse 35 onwards). Christ, 'the bread of life', is a gift from God so wonderful that even the great apostle Paul searched for adjectives to describe him: 'Thanks be to God for his indescribable gift!' (2 Cor. 9:15).

Confronted with these hostile Jews, Christ emphatically asserts his divinity. The words 'I am' (John 6:35) are reminiscent of Exodus 3:14: 'God said to Moses, "I AM WHO I AM. This is what you are to say to the Israelites: I AM has sent me to you."' To quote Mahan again: 'The use of this title by our Lord Jesus Christ at once identifies him as Jehovah of the Old Testament and confirms his deity.'[6]

The manna from heaven

In John 6 Jesus draws several instructive contrasts between the bread in the desert and himself, the true bread.

1. Bread for eternal life. The bread given to the 5,000 and the manna in the wilderness was the 'food that spoils'; it was soon stale and therefore inedible. If kept overnight, the manna stank and bred worms. The Lord gave two days' quota on Friday mornings and miraculously preserved the Sabbath Day's portion overnight. Christ himself is 'food that endures to eternal life' (verse 27). He feeds the immortal soul not just the dying body. People spend so much time, energy and money to buy food for the body and to gain the fleeting pleasures of this life. 'Work for food which gives eternal life', says Jesus.

Just as the Jews had to collect their daily ration of manna, so we too must exert ourselves to gain spiritual manna. Salvation is God's gift but we receive it as we read his Word, listen to preaching, seek him in prayer, repent of our sin and trust in Christ. Those who are lazy concerning their souls go hungry, just as those in the desert went hungry who did not search for God's provision. On another occasion, Jesus spoke about entering a door, rather than eating, to make the same point: 'Make every effort to enter through the narrow door' (Luke 13:24). Do not dither outside the door of conversion – go through it!

2. Bread for the world. In John 6:32-33 Christ calls himself 'the true bread from heaven ... who comes down from heaven and gives life to the world'. Why does Jesus call himself the 'true bread'? He is not merely a substance, like manna, but a living person. This bread lives! Christianity is more than belief in a creed or the practice of certain rituals; it is to know Jesus Christ, the Son of God. The manna gave food for one group (the Jews) in one place (the desert) for a limited period (forty years) – then it finished. The 'true bread ... gives life to the world'; he is food for whoever comes to him regardless of their ethnic origins or social status. He is the 'true bread' as much now as he was 2,000 years ago when he walked the streets of Galilee.

3. *Bread that satisfies for ever.* Christ highlights another contrast: 'I am the bread of life. He who comes to me will never go hungry, and he who believes in me will never be thirsty' (verse 35). The Jews who ate the manna and drank the water from the rock soon felt hungry and thirsty again whereas Jesus gives satisfaction, contentment, joy and peace that continue beyond the grave and last for ever. For forty years, the manna never failed; Christ 'the bread of life' never fails. Christians are never hungry and never thirsty because Christ satisfies, yet still they 'hunger and thirst for righteousness' (Matt. 5:6) because they want to know the Lord better. The contrast is extended when we consider that the Jews ate manna and died, whereas those who repent of their sins will never die (verses 48-51). Christians escape the everlasting death of separation from God (Rom. 6:23) because Christ died in their place on the cross, 'This bread is my flesh, which I give for the life of the world' (verse 51). To give his flesh means to offer himself as an atonement for sin.

4. *Bread for eating.* There are some significant words in verse 51 elaborated in verses 53-58: 'If anyone eats of this bread, he will live for ever.' The key word is *eats.* Each one of the hungry Jews in the wilderness had to eat the quails and manna every day to prevent death. So we too, as individuals, eat of Christ's

body and drink of his blood: 'Jesus said to them, "I tell you the truth, unless you eat the flesh of the Son of Man and drink his blood, you have no life in you. Whoever eats my flesh and drinks my blood has eternal life, and I will raise him up at the last day. For my flesh is real food and my blood is real drink"' (verses 53-55). Jesus was not talking about the literal eating and drinking of his body and blood, an abhorrent idea to any self-respecting Jew (Lev. 17:10-12), neither was he talking about the Lord's Supper, not yet instituted. Rather he is using figurative language, stressing union with himself through faith. Food is necessary for nourishment, so faith is the essence of a personal experience of Christ. We do not merely know about him, we trust him for the pardon of our sins and receive eternal life from him. We have eternal life because Christ is in us. To quote the apostle Paul, 'I have been crucified with Christ and I no longer live, but Christ lives in me. The life I live in the body, I live by faith in the Son of God, who loved me and gave himself for me' (Gal. 2:20). Because Christ lives in us we escape eternal death and will rise from the grave, together with all other believers at the end of the world (John 6:54).

To keep our fellowship with Christ vibrant we feed daily on him as the Israelites ate the manna every day. Notice the present tenses in John 6:54,56: 'Whoever *eats* ... and *drinks*'. The manna 'tasted like wafers made with honey' (Exod. 16:31). Is Christ and his Word sweeter than honey to you? (see Ps. 19:10; Ps. 119:103; Ezek. 3:3).

The manna stopped falling once the Jews entered Canaan; Christ, the heavenly manna, will fully satisfy us in heaven. Then all the discomforts and dangers of this life will no longer exist: 'he who sits on the throne will spread his tent over them. Never again will they hunger; never again will they thirst. The sun will not beat upon them, nor any scorching heat. For the Lamb at the centre of the throne will be their shepherd; he will lead them to springs of living water. And God will wipe away every tear from their eyes' (Rev. 7:15-17).

The mercy seat

We read about manna in two other New Testament passages. One of these is Hebrews 9:4 where we read about the ark of the covenant in the tabernacle that 'contained the gold jar of manna'. The ark was a small chest of acacia wood with a golden lid placed in the most sacred place, 'The holy of holies', which was entered by the high priest only once a year on the day of atonement. The lid of the ark was known as the 'atonement cover' or 'mercy seat'. In this sacred place, God met with Moses, as the representative of his people (Exod. 25:17-22). As we will see in a later chapter, the ark of the covenant is a remarkable picture of the Lord Jesus Christ. The 'jar of manna', kept inside the ark and preserved by God from perishing, reminded God's wandering people of his faithfulness to them for forty years. We too ought to recall past mercies to encourage us to trust God now and in the future. 'The bread of life' will provide our needs whatever the future holds.

The hidden manna

There is an intriguing mention of manna in the last book of the Bible, 'To him who overcomes, I will give some of the hidden manna' (Rev. 2:17). These are Christ's words, from his throne in heaven, to the church at Pergamum in Asia Minor. A member of this church, Antipas, had died as a martyr; others were facing intense temptations and severe trials. It appears that some members had joined the cult of the idolatrous and immoral Nicolaitans, though remaining in church membership. To faithful members who refused to eat at the idol feasts Christ promised 'hidden manna'. Christ would feed them himself. What is this 'hidden manna'? This 'refers to the sufficiency of Christ for the believer's needs, as manna was for the Hebrews during the wilderness wanderings'.[7] It is 'hidden' from unbelievers because they do not know the Saviour.

Richard Brooks says (in his Welwyn Commentary on Revelation), that 'the hidden manna' is 'the enjoyment of meditating upon His glory, of enjoying Him in the assembly of the saints meeting for worship or meeting with Him on our own in the secret place. And all this enjoyment of Christ is but a foretaste of and preparation for enjoying Him in the glory of heaven itself.'[8] Are you looking forward, with eager anticipation, to the everlasting wedding feast of Christ the Lamb? (Rev. 19:5-9).

8.
Christ the Rock
—— (Exod. 17) ——

Paul gives us the key to unlock Exod. 17. In 1 Cor. 10, the apostle identifies the Rock from which the Israelites drank as Christ and cautions the Corinthians not to behave like the Israelites who tested God by their grumbling. The theme of Christ the Rock is found in many Scriptures, for example, Psalm 118:22-24, Isaiah 8:14-15, Daniel 2:1-48, Matt. 21:33-46, Acts 4:10-11 and 1 Peter 2:4-8. Water is also a symbol in the Bible, for example in John 3, 4, and 7, where Jesus compares himself and the Holy Spirit to living water.

God's patience with his petulant people is seen several times in the section from Exodus 15:22 to 17:7. The gracious God turns bitter water into sweet water at Marah, and then leads them to 'Elim, where there were twelve springs and seventy palm trees' so 'they camped there near the water' (15:27). Moving on at God's command into the Desert of Sin, 'the whole community grumbled against Moses and Aaron' because they had no food to eat (16:2-3). Again God showed kindness in sending them manna and quails, provision that lasted 'until they reached the border of Canaan' forty years later (16:35). The grumbling continued when the Hebrews 'camped at Rephidim' where 'there was no water for the people to drink. So they quarrelled with Moses and said, "Give us water to drink"' (17:1-2). In fairness to the complainers, we ought to say that some of their belligerence arose because of anxiety for their children and livestock (verse 3). At Marah, there was bitter water whereas at Rephidim, there was no water; neither situation was a problem for the almighty God.

Had the Hebrews not seen enough of God's power – the Red Sea crossing and his provision so far – to trust God rather than grumble against him? How could they doubt that God was among them? (17:7). Despite the Israelites' peevishness, God showed the rebels mercy by giving them water from a rock (verses 2,6).

Testing the Lord

What is the meaning of Moses' question, 'Why do you put the LORD to the test?' (verse 2). Keil and Delitzsch define this testing the Lord as 'unbelieving doubt in the gracious presence of the Lord to help them.'[1] Their complaining showed ingratitude to God and therefore they were in danger of provoking his wrath.

We are not surprised at Moses' exasperation in verse 4: 'What am I to do with these people? They are almost ready to stone me.' The people had forgotten Moses' competent leadership in the past. Rather than becoming angry with the grumblers, Moses seeks comfort and guidance from God. The Lord does not fail him, or his people. He commands Moses to take 'the staff with which you struck the Nile and go. I will stand there before you by the rock at Horeb. Strike the rock, and water will come out of it for the people to drink' (verses 5-6). To Moses, fearing that the people were about to stone him, God says 'I will stand before you by the rock at Horeb' – the place where God had spoken to the prophet at the burning bush (verse 6).

Some commentators see in the words 'I will stand there before you' (verse 6) a theophany, a visible appearance of the pre-incarnate Christ. It certainly indicates 'the gracious assistance of God' and 'frequently denotes the attitude of a servant when standing before his master, to receive and execute his commands. Thus, Jehovah condescended to come to the help of Moses, and assist His people with His almighty power.'[2]

When Moses struck the rock, water came flowing out to refresh God's people, enough water for over two million people! The Psalmist looks back to this event: 'He split the rocks in the desert and gave them water as abundant as the seas; he brought streams out of a rocky crag and made water flow down like rivers.' God 'turned the rock into a pool, the hard rock into springs of water' (Ps. 78:15-16; 114:8). 'The very rod that had struck the Nile river to deprive Egypt of water (7:14-25) now becomes a source of benefit to the people of Israel by providing water for them.'[3] Naming the place, Masseh ('testing') and Meribah ('quarrelling') 'was so that the people of Israel should never forget how foolishly and shamefully they had acted here.'[4]

Spiritual food and drink

Writing to first-century Christians, the apostle Paul identifies the Rock from which the Israelites drank as the Lord Jesus Christ and cautions the Corinthians not to test the Lord by grumbling against him (1 Cor. 10:4,9-10). Paul gives us the key to unlock Exodus 17.

What does Paul mean by 'spiritual food' and 'spiritual drink'? They ate physical food and drank physical water, but this came from God. The word 'spiritual' points not only to the source of the food and drink but also to the fact that this provision has spiritual significance. 'Just as the Israelites ate spiritual food in the desert, the manna, and they drank from the rock at Rephidim, so we can feed and drink from Christ who is our spiritual rock.'[5] We feed on Christ as we read his Word and listen attentively when it is preached.

The Rock

When Paul writes 'the spiritual rock that accompanied them' (verse 4), he does not mean, as some Jewish teachers taught, that an actual rock followed the Jews throughout the wilderness wanderings. His point is that Christ was with his people, caring for them, as they travelled towards the promised land. Sadly, because of their sins, all but two of those who came out of Egypt (Joshua and Caleb) died in the wilderness (verse 5). Paul sees these events of history as 'examples ... written down as warnings for us ... So, if you think you are standing firm, be careful that you don't fall!' (verses 11-12).

In 1 Corinthians 10:4, the Greek word Paul uses for rock is 'not *petros,* a large stone or boulder but *petra*, a massive rock cliff'.[6] The Rock who protected and sustained the Israelites in the wilderness cares and provides for believers now. He will allow no one to destroy his church or snatch individual Christians from his hands (Matt. 16:18; John 10:28-29). Christ the Rock is strong enough to bear all the problems we bring to him in prayer. He gives us security in the storms of life (Matt. 7:24-27).

In depicting Christ as the Rock, Paul is reiterating Old Testament writers such as David, Isaiah and Daniel. Let's consider three passages that develop this theme.

Psalm 118:22-24. 'The stone the builders rejected has become the capstone; the LORD has done this, and it is marvellous in our eyes. This is the day the LORD has made; let us rejoice and be glad in it.' Who is the rejected stone? Jesus names himself in 'The Parable of the Tenants' as the Stone and the builders as the Jewish leaders who would nail him to a cross. Peter picks up the same Scripture when preaching before the Sanhedrin: 'Jesus Christ of Nazareth, whom you crucified but whom God raised from the dead ... He is "the stone you builders rejected."' His mention of Christ's resurrection suggests that 'the day the Lord has made' is specifically the day that Christ rose from the dead. The apostle cites Psalm 118 again in the second chapter of his first letter. Christ is the Stone rejected by men but precious to God, who raised him from the dead. He is also a precious Stone to believers, but a destructive Stone for those who will not believe and therefore fall over him into hell. He is the foundation Stone of 'a spiritual house', the church (Matt. 21:33-46; Acts 4:10-11; 1 Peter 2:4-8; cf. Eph. 2:19-22). Peter divides the human race into two groups: those 'who believe' and those 'who do not believe'. Either we find Christ a precious Stone or he is a stone over which we fall to eternal damnation.

Isaiah 8:14-15. 'The LORD Almighty ... will be a stone that causes men to stumble and a rock that makes them fall.' Peter's citation of these words in 1 Peter 2:8 shows that 'The LORD Almighty' is Jesus Christ. The apostle in that chapter also quotes Isaiah 28:16, 'This is what the sovereign LORD says: "See, I lay in Zion, a tested stone, a precious cornerstone for a sure foundation; the one who trusts will never be dismayed."' Isaiah 28:16 is also referred to by Paul in Romans 9:32-33 and a similar idea must have been in the mind of the aged Simeon, when he saw the baby Jesus and predicted that 'This child is destined to cause the falling and rising of many in Israel, and to be a sign that will be spoken against' (Luke 2:34).

Daniel 2:1-48. Nebuchadnezzar, king of Babylon, sees in a dream 'a large statue' that is 'enormous', 'dazzling' and 'awesome in appearance' with a golden head, silver chests and arms, thighs of bronze with legs and feet a mixture of iron and baked clay. Then he sees 'a rock ... cut out, but not by human hands' that 'struck the statue on its feet of iron and clay and smashed them' causing the huge statue to collapse. This small rock 'became a huge mountain and filled the whole earth'. Daniel explains to the king that the statue represents four kingdoms and the rock represents 'a kingdom that will never be destroyed' that will bring all other kingdoms to an end 'but it will itself endure forever'. The four kingdoms are Babylon, Persia, Greece and Rome. It was during the period of the Roman Empire that 'a Stone without origin came into this world. He was without origin because he existed before time ... The eternal Son of God came as the insignificant Babe of Bethlehem, to establish an everlasting kingdom. Today the previous kingdoms lie in dust. But Christ's kingdom remains and is growing and will last forever. It will never have a successor. Everything has happened as Daniel said it would.'[7] Daniel's words came true because he spoke God's words to the puzzled king. Christ is the King of kings and Lord of lords to whom every knee will bow and to whom every tongue will confess that he is Lord. He is the 'Lord God Almighty' who reigns forever (Rev. 19:5,16; Phil. 2:9-11).

The Water

Coming back to Exodus 17, we read that water came out of the rock that Moses hit with his rod (verse 6). Christ is not only 'the spiritual rock'; he is also 'the spiritual drink' (1 Cor. 10:4).

Jesus said to the woman of Samaria who came to draw water from Jacob's well: 'Everyone who drinks this water will be thirsty again, but whoever drinks the water I give him will never thirst. Indeed, the water I give him will become in him a spring of water welling up to eternal life' (John 4:13-14). What is this living water? 'In the mind of Christ fresh and pure and never-ceasing spring water was a symbol of everlasting life or salvation.'[8]

Water is also a biblical symbol for the Holy Spirit; he gives the believer a new birth and lives in his soul (John 3:5-8). Again, we recall Jesus' words, '"If anyone is thirsty, let him come to me and drink. Whoever believes in me, as the Scripture has said, streams of living water will flow from within him." By this he meant the Spirit, whom those who believed in him were later to receive. Up to that time the Spirit had not been given, since Jesus had not yet been glorified' (John 7:37-39). Jesus' glorification took place when he returned to heaven; then he gave the Holy Spirit to his church, once for all on the day of Pentecost. Now every believer receives the Holy Spirit at conversion (Acts 2:1-13; Rom. 8:9).

Commenting on Jesus' promise that 'living water will flow from within him', Hendriksen writes: 'Those who drink from the Fountain, Christ, receive lasting satisfaction for themselves – everlasting life, salvation full and free – but in addition ... they become by God's sovereign grace, a channel of abundant blessings to others. The church proclaims the message of salvation to the world, so that the elect from every clime and nation are gathered in.'[9]

Jesus' teaching in John chapters 3, 4 and 7, echoes God's promise through Ezekiel: 'I will sprinkle clean water on you, and you will be clean; I will cleanse you from all impurities and from all your idols. I will give you a new heart and put a new spirit in you; I will remove from you your heart of stone and give you a heart of flesh. And I will put my Spirit in you and move you to follow my decrees and be careful to keep my laws' (Ezek. 36:25-27). The Holy Spirit sprinkling clean water, giving a new heart and a new spirit, is his work of regeneration – the new birth. The Holy Spirit moving the believer to keep God's law is his work of sanctification – holiness. The Holy Spirit will never leave the true child of God; he is with him and in him for ever to glorify the Lord Jesus Christ (John 14:17; 16:14). Christ is the Lamb and Shepherd who in heaven will lead believers 'to springs of living water' and will 'wipe away every tear from their eyes' (Rev. 7:17).

Are you building your life on the Rock, the Lord Jesus Christ? Are you so full of the Water, Christ and his Spirit, that you must tell others about him? If you can honestly answer yes to these questions then you will see the Lamb who is also the Shepherd in heaven.

9.

Christ gives rest
—— (Exod. 17-18) ——

The generation that left Egypt, except for Joshua and Caleb, perished in the wilderness because of their unbelief. The writer to the Hebrews takes up this subject of God's people missing his rest because of their unbelief. In Heb. 3, he compares and contrasts Moses with Jesus. Christ is God's Son and therefore greater than Moses who is only a servant (though an important one) in God's house, the church. We enter God's rest by trusting Christ for salvation. The ultimate rest for believers is heaven. Only those who 'hear his voice' will enjoy the 'promised land' of heaven. Jesus promised rest to those who submit to his yoke – his will (Matt. 11:28-30).

Soon after the dramatic Red Sea crossing – the victory song hardly finished – the Israelites are grumbling. They grumble about the bitter waters of Marah and then they complain about lack of food and water in the wilderness. How does the Lord respond to their complaints? As we have seen, he makes the bitter water sweet and provides daily quails and manna (Exod. 15:22-17:7). However, even God's patience has its limits and therefore, he sent a plague and snakes to punish his disobedient people (Num. 16; 21:4-9). Nevertheless, he mixes wrath with mercy – all who look to the brass snake on a pole receive physical healing. The uplifted snake is a picture of the uplifted Saviour – all who look to him receive spiritual healing (John 3:14-15).

This continual murmuring was caused by unbelief. The generation that left Egypt, apart from Joshua and Caleb, perished in the wilderness because of this unbelief. Sadly, the children of this first generation also spent much of their time complaining against God and his servant, Moses. The writer to the Hebrews, in the third and fourth chapters of his letter, takes up this theme of God's people missing his rest because of their unbelief.

Jesus greater than Moses

The author of Hebrews begins his third chapter by comparing and contrasting Moses and Jesus. Why? Because some of the Hebrews were abandoning Christ and returning to Moses. Christ is not only greater than prophets and angels (Heb. 1-2); he is also greater than Moses. What is the antidote for apostasy? 'Fix your thoughts on Jesus, the apostle and high priest' (Heb. 3:1).

Both Moses and Jesus served God faithfully though they faced opposition and obstacles. Nothing deterred Moses or Christ from the path of loyal obedience to God. So what is the difference between Moses and Christ? Moses was not faultless as the incident in Numbers 20 clearly shows. He snapped in fury as he lost his temper with God's people (verse 10). As a result, God said 'you will not bring this community into the land that I give them.' Christ is the only perfect leader. He alone is free from sin (Heb. 7:26). This contrast between sinful Moses and the sinless Christ is implied rather than explicitly stated in Hebrews 3.

Moses and Christ were both 'faithful in all God's house' (Heb. 3:2). God's house is not a building of bricks and mortar but people who belong to God. 'In the Old Testament it was primarily the nation of Israel, but now it is the Christian church, the whole family of converted people. Some are already in heaven and others are still on earth.'[1] Moses and Christ have different positions in God's house: Moses is God's servant, Christ is God's Son; Moses belonged to a household, Christ built a household; Moses is a labourer, Christ is the architect. He is God the builder of his church (Heb. 3:2-5, see also 1:1-3,8). He built his church by his death; those for whom he died are his children (2:14).

Jesus is the One to whom Moses pointed – this is the meaning of the phrase 'testifying to what would be said in the future' (3:5). 'Moses is a type of Christ, a human analogy of the incarnate Son … Moses cared for Israel as a servant in the house of God. But Christ cares for (and rules over) the church as the Son and heir. The picture is that of a great household, created by the Father through the Son, and inherited by the Son.'[2] Evidence that we are in God's house is that 'we hold on to our courage and the hope of which we boast' (verse 6). Perseverance proves profession!

'Hear his voice'

The rest of Hebrews 3, and on into chapter 4, expands the warning of 3:6 taking Psalm 95:7-11 as the starting point because it refers to the Israelites in the wilderness. The words 'time of testing' (Heb. 3:8) refer to the events at Rephidim where the Israelites quarrelled with Moses because there was no water. After water flowed from a rock, Moses called the place Massah, a name that means 'testing' (Exod. 17:1-7). 'Do not test the Lord like your ancestors' is the message of Psalm 95. Testing God by persistently refusing to 'hear his voice' leads to an 'unbelieving heart' that is 'hardened by sin's deceitfulness' – these are symptoms of 'unbelief'. Unbelief prevents entrance into God's rest (Heb. 3:12-13,16-19).

The Israelites heard God's voice promising them a homeland (Deut. 1:8). 'The analogy is clear. The recipients of Hebrews had heard and welcomed a greater promise – the promise of the gospel. They had heard a greater call – to possess salvation and eternal glory through faith in Christ alone. Would they now turn their backs on that gospel, as the Israelites forsook the promised land and perished in the wilderness when their hearts became discouraged? (Deut. 1:27-28).'[3] So now, 'those who dabble in the gospel, but never really obey its command to repent and believe on Christ, can never know eternal rest.'[4]

Rest

What, then, is God's rest? To enter God's rest is to 'hear his voice' (Heb. 3:7). We hear his voice when we hear, and respond to, the gospel. Those who believe enter God's rest (Heb. 4:2-3). Disobedience shuts the door into God's rest (4:6). The person who 'enters God's rest also rests from his own work' (verse 10). Entering God's rest is trusting in Christ for salvation. We give up trying to save ourselves and depend on Christ alone. The ultimate rest for God's people is heaven. Only those who 'hear his voice' will enjoy the 'promised land' of heaven.

The Israelites, living about 2,000 years before Christ, heard Moses preach the gospel! (verse 2). How did Moses proclaim the gospel to the Israelites in the wilderness? By the Passover, the crossing of the Red Sea, the water from the rock, the symbolism of the tabernacle, priesthood and sacrifices besides the commandments revealing their sin and need of a Saviour. However, most of the Jews missed the meaning of these things – as did the readers of Hebrews – because 'they were putting their trust in the external symbols of the old covenant rather than in the Christ symbolised.'[5]

Commenting on the word 'disobey' in Hebrews 3:18, Philip Arthur explains that it describes the Israelites' rejection of God over a long period. 'They were not being condemned for a momentary lapse. They had resisted the Lord at every turn. They were chronically disobedient, so much so that it made their claim to faith look shallow.'[6] They refused to 'hear his voice' and therefore they did not enter into the promised land.

Invitation

Are you burdened with the guilt of sin? Accept Jesus' gracious invitation: 'Come to me, all you who are weary and burdened, and I will give you rest. Take my yoke upon you and learn from me, for I am gentle and humble in heart, and you will find rest for your souls. For my yoke is easy and my burden is light' (Matt. 11:28-30). The real Christian submits to God's will – 'take my yoke' – and is teachable – 'learn from me'. Are you a true Christian or only a 'temporary believer' like so many of the Israelites in the wilderness? 'May we never be satisfied till we know and feel that we have come to Christ by faith for rest, and do still come to Him for fresh supplies of grace every day! If we have come to Him already, let us learn to cleave to Him more closely. If we have never come to Him yet, let us begin to come today.'[7]

10.
Christ fulfils the law
——— (Exod. 20) ———

We ought to read Exodus 20:1-17 alongside Matthew chapters 5-7. Christ fulfilled the law (Matt. 5:17) by explaining the true meaning of the law, obeying the Law, and taking the punishment demanded by the law for transgressors. The Ten Commandments define sin and show us our need of the Saviour. Moses acted as the mediator for the frightened Hebrews (Exod. 20:18-21). Christ is our Mediator and Advocate who speaks to God on our behalf. Exodus 20 links to several NT texts, including Matt. 22:34-40, Rom. 7, Gal. 3 and Heb. 12:18-24. Jesus in the Sermon on the Mount uses the Ten Commandments to describe the conduct of the Christian.

'Teacher ... all these I have kept since I was a boy' a rich Jewish young man replied when Jesus quoted to him six of the Ten Commandments. He smugly praised himself because he had not committed murder, adultery and theft. He spoke truthfully to everyone and treated his parents with respect. Jesus' words wiped the self-satisfied smile from his face: 'Go, sell everything you have and give to the poor, and you will have treasure in heaven. Then come follow me.' What happened next? 'He went away sad, because he had great wealth.' He loved his money more than he loved God – he had broken the first commandment, 'You shall have no other gods before me' (Mark 10:17-23; Exod. 20:3). He valued possessions more than his eternal soul.

The young man claimed to have kept from childhood at least five of the Ten Commandments. Commentators debate the meaning of the word 'defraud' (Mark 10:19). Is this a reference to the tenth commandment, 'You shall not covet' (Exod. 20:17)? 'When a person covets the goods belonging to another, does he not in heart and mind defraud the neighbour of that which belongs to him?'[1] He defrauded the poor by his refusal to sell everything to provide for them.

He came to Jesus with the wrong question, 'What must I *do* to inherit eternal life?' Better to ask, 'How may I *receive* eternal life?' There's an eternity of difference between doing and receiving. We cannot climb to heaven by the ten-rung ladder of the law – the holy God never intended that we should! Why then did Jesus quote the Commandments to the rich young man? To show him his need of a Saviour.

(Christ's key)

In the Sermon on the Mount, Jesus puts in our hands the key to unlock the meaning of the Ten Commandments given to Moses on Mount Sinai. We ought to read Exodus 20:1-17 alongside Matthew chapters 5-7.

Matthew 5:17-18 is pivotal in Christ's sermon because in these verses he reveals his own view of the Old Testament: 'Do not think that I have come to abolish the Law or the Prophets; I have not come to abolish them but to fulfil them.' The term 'the Law or the Prophets' covers the entire Old Testament. In this verse Jesus 'dismisses the charge of his enemies that he is a proclaimer of novelties, and shows that his ministry was not in collision with the Old Testament but in harmony with it; in fact without him the Old Testament was incomplete, unfulfilled.'[2] How does Christ fulfil the law and the prophets? By explaining the true meaning of the law and enforcing his teaching by obedience; by fulfilling the Old Testament types and predictions and by taking the punishment demanded by the law for transgressors. Verse 18 means that 'not in the slightest respect will the Old Testament remain unfulfilled. It is as if we were to say that with respect to its fulfilment "not a 't' will remain uncrossed and not an 'i' undotted.'"[3] The words 'I have come' (verse 17) reveal Jesus' awareness of his Messianic mission and his pre-existence – he has come from God's presence in heaven to do God's will on earth, in fulfilment of God's Word.

The purpose of the law

Jesus teaches in the Sermon on the Mount that God demands more than outward conformity to the law. He looks at the desires of the heart. Our obedience must surpass the strict moral behaviour of the Pharisees – they are like cups that are clean on the outside but dirty inside with 'greed and self-indulgence' (Matt. 5:20; 23:25). The command 'do not murder' is not confined to the physical taking of a life, it includes angry contempt and an unforgiving spirit. We may murder a person's reputation by our words. Likewise, the command 'do not commit adultery' extends to lustful looking and impure thinking (Exod. 20:13-14; Matt. 5:21-30). Jesus' teaching is anticipated in the tenth commandment, 'you shall not covet', which reveals that God is concerned with the attitudes of our hearts.

The boastful rich young man possessed an inadequate and superficial understanding of God's law. He had not grasped that salvation is not through the law – neither had Paul understood this truth until his conversion on the Damascus road. However, in Romans and Galatians he emphatically states that God does not save us because of law keeping. We read, for example, 'No-one will be declared righteous in his sight by observing the law; rather, through the law we become conscious of sin' and 'No-one is justified before God by the law' (Rom. 3:20; Gal. 3:11). Furthermore, he teaches that sinners hate God and his law: 'the sinful mind is hostile to God. It does not submit to God's law, nor can it do so. Those controlled by the sinful nature cannot please God.' Such rebellion deserves death, 'The wages of sin is death' (Rom. 8:7-8; 6:23).

Why did God give the Ten Commandments to Moses at Mount Sinai? To bring conviction of sin. Paul's own experience proves the point: 'I would not have known what sin was except through the law. For I would not have known what coveting really was if the law had not said, "Do not covet." But sin, seizing the opportunity afforded by the commandment, produced in me every kind of covetous desire.' Once Paul knew the law – 'you shall not covet' – his sinful heart became more covetous! We rebel against prohibitions. The problem is not with the law but with sin within us: 'The law is holy, and the commandment is holy, righteous and good' (Rom. 7:7-12). An evidence of conversion is that, like Paul, we now love God's law: 'For in my inner being I delight in God's law' (verse 22).

God's law not only defines sin and convicts the sinner; it sends him to the only Saviour, the Lord Jesus Christ. 'We were held prisoners by the law, locked up until faith should be revealed. So the law was put in charge to lead us to Christ that we might be justified by faith' (Gal. 3:23-24). The words 'put in charge' translate the Greek word, *paidagōgos*, – the servant who took Jewish boys to school.[4] The *paidagōgos* often exercised severe discipline so that those placed under his guardianship longed for the freedom they would receive when they became adults. Who are the 'prisoners' held 'by the law'? They are Old Testament believers waiting for the coming of the Messiah-Saviour. The experience of Old Testament believers has a parallel in the emotions of the sinner under conviction of sin. The law condemns and makes him feel guilty so that he longs for freedom from sin's guilt and power. Christ alone brings spiritual liberty!

What place does the law have in the life of the believer?[5] Do we express our obedience to God by adhering to the Ten

Commandments? Let's put that question in another way: to whom was Jesus speaking in the Sermon on the Mount? The question is answered in Matthew 5:1-2: 'Now when he saw the crowds, he went up on a mountainside and sat down. His *disciples* came to him, and he began to teach *them*' (italics mine). The Lord was primarily teaching his disciples, though 'the crowds' listened as well! Christ the King described the character (5:3-12) and the conduct (5:13-7:28) of the citizens of his kingdom. He addressed his teaching on the law to his disciples. Dr. Martyn Lloyd-Jones explains the purpose of Christ's sermon: 'We are not told in the Sermon on the Mount, "Live like this and you will become a Christian"; rather we are told, "Because you are a Christian live like this." This is how Christians ought to live; this is how Christians are meant to live.'[6]

God said to Moses at Sinai, 'Now if you obey me fully and keep my covenant, then out of all nations you will be my treasured possession. Although the whole earth is mine, you will be for me a kingdom of priests and a holy nation' (Exod. 19:5-6). We have an echo of these words in 1 Peter 2:9. 'God speaks in the same way to the Christian church as he did to the Jews ... These Commandments are what is expected of the people who belong to God, whoever they are and wherever they are.'[7]

Who spoke at Sinai? The LORD, Christ, who declared to Moses at the burning bush, 'I am the LORD your God' (Exod. 20:2; 3:14).[8] Therefore, Jesus speaking as the divine lawgiver says in the Sermon of Mount, 'You have heard ... but I tell you' (Matt. 5:21-22,27-28,31-32,33-34,38-39,43-44). Erudite rabbis quoted authorities to support their conflicting views. Jesus said 'I tell you' because he spoke as God, whose commands are binding on all in every age and for every culture. Matthew comments on the reaction to Jesus' sermon: 'When Jesus had finished saying these things, the crowds were amazed at his teaching, because he taught as one who had authority, and not as their teachers of the law' (7:28-29). 'They listened spell-bound to the end and were left amazed' with 'a buzz of astonishment'. The verb means literally that they 'were struck out of themselves'.[9]

Christ obeys the law

Commenting on the word 'fulfil' in Matthew 5:17, Brian Edwards says, 'The most natural understanding of this verse is that the whole life of Christ is a summary of obedience to the law of God. We watch him to see what obedience to the law means. When we come to some difficult application in our modern society we must ask: "How would Christ have obeyed the law at this point?"'[10]

Christ obeyed the law as the representative of his elect; his obedience reached its climax in his atoning death on the cross. In Romans 5, Paul compares Adam and Christ ('the last Adam'[11]): Adam representing the human race disobeyed God and brought death and condemnation; Christ representing the elect obeyed God and brought life and justification. In Adam, we are declared guilty; in Christ, we are declared not guilty. To quote Paul, 'For just as through the disobedience of the one man the many were made sinners, so also through the obedience of the one man the many will be made righteous' (Rom. 5:19). To obey God, Christ obeyed God's law.

Christ condemned by the law

We read in Galatians 3, 'Christ redeemed us from the curse of the law by becoming a curse for us, for it is written: "Cursed is everyone who is hung on a tree"' (verse 13). Lawbreakers deserve God's eternal wrath (Rom. 1:18, 6:23). Nonetheless, God laid on Christ our iniquity; he bore God's wrath against penitent sinners (Isaiah 53:5-6,10-12). God declares us not guilty because he declared his sinless Son guilty in our place.

To support his statement that Christ became a curse for us, Paul cites Deuteronomy 21:23. Hendriksen explains this quote and its relevance to the apostle's argument: 'In its Old

Testament context … this passage does not refer to death by crucifixion, which was not known among the Israelites as a mode of capital punishment. It refers instead, to the custom according to which after a wrong-doer had been executed, his dead body was nailed to a post or tree. But if, in the sight of God, the hanging of a *dead* body was a curse, how much more would not the slow, painful, and shameful death by crucifixion of a living person be a curse, especially when that dying one was experiencing anguish beyond the power of description!'[12] Christ, bearing the law's curse and God's wrath, cries out on the cross, 'My God, my God, why have you forsaken me?' (Matt. 27:46).

The Mediator

Moses describes Israel's reaction to the scene at Mount Sinai: 'When the people saw the thunder and lightning and heard the trumpet and saw the mountain in smoke, they trembled with fear. They stayed at a distance and said to Moses, "Speak to us yourself and we will listen. But do not have God speak to us or we will die." Moses said to the people, "Do not be afraid. God has come to test you, so that the fear of God will be with you to keep you from sinning." The people remained at a distance, while Moses approached the thick darkness where God was' (Exod. 20:18-21). Why were the people afraid? Because they knew that they were in the presence of a holy God and that they were law-breaking sinners deserving his wrath. Nevertheless, God had not spoken at Sinai to destroy the Israelites but to test them – would they keep their promise to 'do everything the LORD has said'? (Exod. 19:8). A true fear of God always leads to wholehearted obedience (20:20).

'Moses, you speak to us instead of God', the terrified Israelites implored Moses who took on the role of the covenant mediator. We may come near to God, rather than stay at a distance like the Israelites, because the Lord Jesus Christ, our Mediator, paid our debt to the law by dying on the cross.

In the final section of Exodus 20, God tells Moses to build an altar of earth and uncut stones for 'burnt offerings and fellowship offerings' (verses 22-26). 'The altar through which we come near to God was made, not of earth and stone, but of plain, rough-hewn wood which had quickly been put together in the form of *a cross*.'[13]

'The church of the firstborn'

The writer to the Hebrews contrasts the frightened Israelites at Mount Sinai and joyful Christians who 'have come to Mount Zion, to the heavenly Jerusalem … the church of the firstborn … to Jesus the mediator of the new covenant' (Heb. 12:18-24). The firstborn in a Jewish home occupied a prominent role within the family and received special privileges. Christ is God's firstborn, now enthroned in heaven, the first of many sons to be raised from the dead (Col. 1:15-20; 1 Cor. 15:51-58; Eph. 1:18-23; Phil. 2: 9-11; 3:20-21). Why does the author of Hebrews offer this comparison? 'The answer is given in verse 25. Some people refused the message of God when it was delivered from the earthly mountain … Multitudes of them remained in the wilderness because the way ahead was too demanding. They never entered the rest that God had prepared. If that was the fate of those who would not obey under the old scheme of things, what excuse is available now that God speaks through his Son? The people who closed their ears to God when he spoke from the threatening slopes of Mount Sinai were very foolish. It is even more foolish to close our ears to God when he speaks from the gentle and welcoming slopes of Mount Zion.'[14]

Christ 'the end of the law'

The apostle Paul makes an important statement concerning Christ and the law in Romans 10:4: 'Christ is the end of the law so that there may be righteousness for everyone who believes.' In what sense is Christ 'the end of the law'? Stuart

Olyott paraphrases Paul's point: 'The Jews are ignorant of the one way of getting right with God. They try to earn God's favour *their* way – by earning it through Law-keeping, and so they do not submit to God's revealed way. Christ spells the end of trying to get right with God by keeping the Law, by works or self-effort, by any form of earning, or by personal achievement. The way that Christ has opened is the way of believing.'[15] This text sums up the message of the book of Romans and therefore briefly states the essential gospel: salvation is in Christ alone. He came into the world to save sinners apart from the law (1 Tim. 1:15; Rom. 3:21-22).

Christ sums up the law

'Which is the greatest commandment in the law?' a Pharisee, skilled in the Jewish law, asks Jesus. The Pharisees added to the Mosaic Law 613 commandments, 248 of them positive and 365 negative and endlessly argued about the greatest of these commandments. How would Jesus answer? He sums up God's law in the one word *love*. 'Jesus replied: '"Love the Lord your God with all your heart and with all your soul and with all your mind." This is the first and greatest commandment. And the second is like it: 'Love your neighbour as yourself.' All the Law and the Prophets hang on these two commandments"' (Matt. 22:34-40). To love God we keep Commandments one to four and to love man, as an expression of our love to God, we keep Commandments five to ten. Jesus echoes words well known to the Pharisees (Deut. 6:5; Lev. 19:18). 'This twofold command ... is the peg on which the whole "law and the prophets" hang. Remove that peg, and all is lost, for the entire Old Testament with its commandments and covenants, prophecies and promises, types and testimonies, invitations and exhortations, points to the love of God which demands the answer of love in return.'[16]

11.

Christ the Servant
—————— (Exod. 21) ——————

Christ, like the slave who gained his freedom in the Jubilee Year, declares: 'I love my master ... and do not want to go free.' Placing Exod. 21 alongside Ps. 40, Heb. 10, Isa. 42, 53, Phil. 2 and Eph. 5, we consider Christ the obedient, suffering, loving and selfless servant who gave his life on the cross because of his love to God and his love to his wife, the church. Jesus, in his role as the Messiah, willingly obeyed God as a servant obeyed his master. Christ's devotion to God is a model for us to copy.

Have you ever read a biography of John Newton?[1] If so, you will know something about the evils of the slave trade. Traders hunted men, women and children like animals on the West coast of Africa shipping them across to America. Hundreds of slaves died on the long journey and cruel masters ill-treated the survivors. After his conversion, John Newton, a former slave trader, joined the politician William Wilberforce, an evangelical, in the campaign to abolish this appalling trade.

Newton never forgot his own former bondage to sin and displayed in his study the words of Deuteronomy 15:15, 'Thou shalt remember thou wast a bondman ... the LORD thy God redeemed thee' (AV). These words are in a chapter dealing with the release of Hebrews who sold themselves to fellow-Jews because of debt. The parallel passage in Exodus is chapter 21:1-6, to which we now turn our attention.

God forbade the Jews to kidnap anyone or even to own a kidnapped person; any person caught breaking this law faced death (Exod. 21:16). However, the Jews could take prisoners of war and buy foreign slaves but God expected his people to treat these slaves with kindness. We read in Exodus 21 that a Hebrew in debt might sell himself to a fellow-Hebrew creditor. Such enslaved Jews became hired servants rather than slaves; their condition was much better than the slaves transported to America or the lot of the Jews in Egyptian bondage. In the seventh-year, the Hebrew servant could 'go free, without paying anything' (verse 2). The Jubilee Year brought release for the Hebrew slave irrespective of how many years he had served (Lev. 25:39-43). The freed Hebrew received supplies from the flock, the threshing-floor and the winepress (Deut. 15:12-15). This wonderful provision of the merciful God gave the freed slave another opportunity to make a success of his life.

If the hired servant married before he became a slave, his wife shared his freedom, if he married after becoming a slave then his wife and children could not go free with him. The wife belonged to the master and a servant might therefore choose to give up his freedom (Exod. 21:3-4). 'If the servant declares, "I love my master and my wife and children and do not want to go free," then his master must take him before the judges. He shall take him to the door ... and pierce his ear with an awl. Then he will be his servant for life' (verses 5-6). The awl is a small tool often used nowadays to pierce holes in leather. The pierced ear permanently marked the servant. Perhaps this piercing took place at the door of the city, to show that the door to freedom would remain shut forever to the man with the pierced ear. The slave belonged to the family of his master for the rest of his life.

What relevance has this ancient Jewish custom to present-day Christians? It foreshadows Christ's obedience to his Father and is a picture of the Christian's devotion to Christ, God's servant.

Obedient Servant

A key to unlock Exodus 21 is Hebrews 10:5-7, which is a quotation of the Messianic Psalm 40. The writer to the Hebrews puts the words of Psalm 40 into the mouth of the Lord Jesus Christ: 'sacrifice and offering you did not desire, but my ears you have pierced; burnt offerings and sin offerings you did not require. Then I said, "Here I am, I have come – it is written about me in the scroll. I desire to do your will, O my God; your law is within my heart"' (Ps. 40:6-8).

Sacrifices offered by sinners, however sincere, were always deficient; Christ offered his obedient life and his atoning death as a perfect sacrifice to God. The predominant theme of the letter to the Hebrews is that Christ 'offered for all time one sacrifice for sins' making all the old Jewish sacrifices unnecessary. God freely forgives penitent sinners because of Christ's death, and where sin has been forgiven 'there is no longer any sacrifice for sin' (Heb. 10:12,18).

The words of Psalm 40:6 – 'sacrifice and offering you did not desire, but my ears you have pierced' – suggest a link with the events of Exodus 21. The writer to the Hebrews quotes the Septuagint (the Greek translation of the Hebrew), 'a body you prepared for me' (Heb. 10:5). The literal Hebrew is 'Ears you dug for me.' Harry Uprichard helpfully comments: 'The overall sense is plain: God works in David's life to produce in him a willing obedience, preparing, shaping and moulding him for service. The apostle picks up this theme in his exposition: God's preparation of a body for his Son leads to Christ's willingness to offer his body in sacrifice. Christ's prepared body anticipates his willing obedience in sacrifice. Love to the Father's goodness compels the Son's ready response.'[2]

'I desire to do your will, O my God' (Psalm 40:8) is an apt summary of Christ's life. Just as the Hebrew servant was ready to do whatever his master said and proved his obedience by relinquishing his freedom, symbolised by the pierced ear, so

Christ delighted in God and his Word. He spoke every word and performed every deed in wholehearted obedience to his Father's will. Christ the servant willingly subjected himself to his Father's commands: 'The one who sent me is with me; he has not left me alone, for I always do what pleases him' (John 8:29). From childhood through to death he devoted himself to his 'Father's business' (Luke 2:49, AV).

Christ's willing obedience stands in contrast with Moses' hesitant obedience (Exod. chapters 4-7). Moses says, 'O Lord, please send someone else'; Jesus says 'I desire to do your will, O my God'. Moses says 'O Lord, I have never been eloquent ... I am slow of speech and tongue' and therefore God gives him Aaron to speak on his behalf: 'see I have made you like God to Pharaoh, and your brother Aaron will be your prophet. You are to say everything I command you, and your brother Aaron is to tell Pharaoh to let the Israelites go out of his country' (Exod. 4:10,13; 7:1-2). Just as Moses spoke through Aaron, so God speaks through Christ. He is God's prophet who speaks what the Father commands him (John 7:16). Moses foretold the coming of the divine Prophet and Peter records the fulfilment of this prophecy (Deut. 18:17-19; Acts 3:19-23; cf. Acts 7:37).

Suffering Servant

Christ is the Suffering Servant of Isaiah's prophecy: 'Here is my servant, whom I uphold, my chosen one in whom I delight; I will put my Spirit on him and he will bring justice to the nations' (Isa. 42:1); 'see, my servant will act wisely; he will be raised and lifted up and highly exalted' (Isa. 52:13). Jesus' own view of his ministry looked back to these prophecies: 'The Son of Man did not come to be served, but to serve, and to give his life as a ransom for many' (Mark 10:45). We begin to understand what he meant when we read John 13 and see Jesus, the humble Son of God, washing the feet of his own disciples.

Loving Servant

'I love my master' (Exod. 21:5) expresses Jesus' attitude in eternity before his incarnation at Bethlehem; love to his Father brought him down to earth to die on the cross. When John tells us in the prologue to his Gospel that Jesus, the eternal Word, 'was with God', he is highlighting not only his equality with God and his pre-existence but also the love and companionship which always existed between God and his Son (John 1:1-2). According to William Hendriksen the words 'with God' denote 'face to face with God'. 'The meaning is that the Word existed in the closest possible fellowship with the Father, and that he took supreme delight in this communion ... This fully divine Word, existing from all eternity as a distinct Person, was enjoying loving fellowship with the Father.'[3] This everlasting love between Father and Son forms the backdrop of the Son's obedience to his Father while on earth.

Selfless Servant

Another passage that speaks of Christ the servant is Philippians 2:5-8. Christ, though fully God 'did not think this equality with God a thing to be eagerly grasped or retained. But stripped Himself [of all privileges and rightful dignity] so as to assume the guise of a servant' (Phil. 2:6, Amplified Bible). Charles Wesley employs his poetic skills in an attempt to express what Paul means: 'Our God contracted to a span, incomprehensibly made man.'[4] Just think for a moment of the outcome if Christ had insisted on his own rights – everlasting hell for the entire human race. Instead, he puts the lostness of his elect before his own interests because of his love to his Father. The apostle prefaces this Christological passage with the words 'Your attitude should be the same as that of Christ Jesus' (verse 5). The humble Christian puts the interests of others before his own.

We gain further insights into Christ's obedience to his divine Master as we read the accounts of his earthly life in the four Gospels. Take, for example, the temptation in the wilderness at the beginning of his public ministry (Matt. 4:1-11). We must not think of Jesus' temptation as a charade because of his divinity. After six weeks of fasting, he felt the persuasive force of Satan's suggestion to turn stones into bread. The temptation was a fierce battle that he fought and won. Facing the devil at the end of his ministry, Jesus the man struggled in the garden of Gethsemane with the prospect of an ignominious death, 'even death on a cross!' (Phil. 2:8). The cross for Jews meant disgrace of the worst kind. Will he give up his own freedom and willingly suffer humiliation from wicked men? Will he take the cup of God's wrath against sinners? Would he suffer the pains of hell involving separation for the first time from his heavenly Father? The suffering Servant ignores Satan as he submits voluntarily to his Father's will, saying: 'Not what I will, but what you will' (Mark 14:36). This is the Servant declaring 'I love my master ... and do not want to go free.' So he goes to the cross shutting his ears to the Jewish leaders' derision – 'come down from the cross and save yourself!' (Mark 15:30) – and opening his ears to God's command to die for his people.

'I love my wife'

If it is right to apply the first part of Exodus 21:5 – 'I love my master' – to Christ, how does the second part of this verse – 'I love my wife and my children' – apply to him? The church is Christ's bride (Eph. 5:22-33); the children are individual Christians within the church. The church is the heavenly Jerusalem, the mother of all believers, Jews and non-Jews (Gal. 4:26). It was because 'Christ loved the church' that he 'gave himself up for her to make her holy' (Eph 5:25). So great was his love for his bride that he submitted to a painful and shameful death by crucifixion.

'I love my master'

Exodus 21:1-6 not only foreshadows Christ's obedience, it is also a picture of the Christian's devotion to his heavenly Master. If the Hebrew servant vowed lifelong service to an earthly master, how much more should Christians devote themselves to their Master in heaven? The earthly master accepted six years' service instead of payment of debts; but our gracious Master gave his life to redeem us from spiritual bondage. Surely Calvary's love should move us to respond, 'I love my master ... I do not want to go free.'

The pierced ear identified the slave, and so our changed lives mark us out as the Lord's servants. Are we afraid to stand out from the crowd? Is our lifestyle different from unconverted family and friends? The apostle Paul delighted to call himself 'a servant of Christ Jesus' and told the Roman believers 'I am not ashamed of the gospel, because it is the power of God for the salvation of everyone who believes' (Rom. 1:16). His courage cost him dear; writing to the churches of Galatia he says 'I bear on my body the marks of Jesus' (Gal. 6:17). His scarred back proved his love to Christ just as the pierced ear proved the Hebrew servant's love to his master. Paul, after his beating, still boasted about Christ's death: 'May I never boast except in the cross of our Lord Jesus Christ, through which the world has been crucified to me, and I to the world' (Gal. 6:14). Are we devoted to Christ and his cross or caught up with the attractions of this passing world?

David, while writing prophetically of the coming Messiah in Psalm 40:8, also expressed his own longing to please God: 'I desire to do your will, O my God; your law is within my heart.' Paul takes up David's sentiments in his letter to the Romans, 'in my inner being I delight in God's law' (Rom. 7:22). Both David and Paul, despite sin within, yearned for perfect obedience to God. Both men remembered their failings with tears (Ps. 51; Rom. 7:14-25). Both men rejoiced in God's grace (Ps. 32:1-2; Rom. 3:21-31). This is the normal Christian life!

Why might the Hebrew servant give himself forever to his master? His affirmation tells us, '... the servant declares, "I love my master and my wife and children and do not want to go free"' (Exod. 21:5). The word 'declares' in this verse shows 'all the earnestness and warmth of his heart'.[5] Love oils the wheels of obedience and says, 'I do not want to go free.' The slave affirmed this love for his master publicly 'before the judges' who ensured that he acted freely (verse 5). For the Christian a life of commitment to God proclaims his undying love for Christ his Lord. Leaving his master was simply not an option for the Hebrew servant; it is not an option for the true servant of Christ. To leave Christ is the fast lane to hell.

Francis Ridley Havergal, a 19th century hymn writer, recalls the events of Exodus 21:

> I love, I love my Master,
> I will not go out free!
> For He is my Redeemer;
> He paid the price for me.
> I would not leave His service,
> It is so sweet and blest;
> And in the weariest moments
> He gives the truest rest.
>
> My Master shed His life-blood
> My vassal life to win,
> And save me from the bondage
> Of tyrant self and sin.
> He chose me for His service,
> And gave me power to choose
> That blessed, perfect freedom,
> Which I shall never lose.
>
> I would not halve my service,
> His only it must be!

His only – Who so loved me,
And gave Himself for me.
Rejoicing and adoring,
Henceforth my soul shall be –
I love, I love my Master,
I will not go out free![6]

12.

Christ the Tabernacle
—— (Exod. 25 etc) ——

The starting point for this chapter is John 1:14 where the apostle tells us that Christ dwelt – tabernacled – among us. The tabernacle in the wilderness points to Christ. We look at God's pattern and purpose in instructing Moses to erect the tabernacle and the Israelites' enthusiastic support for this project. The tabernacle situated in the middle of the Israelite camp reminds us that Christ must be at the centre of our lives. Each item in the tabernacle is a type of Christ. When Christ died, God himself tore down the veil that separated the Holy of Holies from the rest of the tabernacle. This action declared that God accepted the once-for-all sacrifice of Christ on behalf of sinners. God welcomes sinners because Christ is our 'mercy-seat'. Believers are now God's tabernacle – God will live among his people for ever (Rev. 21).

Is the tabernacle in the wilderness a picture of the Lord Jesus Christ? Do we have New Testament keys to unlock its symbolism? In the letter to the Hebrews the structure and ritual of the Old Testament tabernacle is a springboard into teaching about Christ the great high priest (Heb. 8-10). The tabernacle points to Christ who '*tabernacled* among us' – this is the meaning of the Greek word translated as 'dwelling' in John 1:14 – 'The Word became flesh and made his dwelling among us.'

John Davis warns against extreme typology when considering the tabernacle: 'It is quite apparent that some parts of the tabernacle were there for only one reason: to give it structural support; they were not intended to convey some mystical typological meaning.'[1] For example, 'there is widespread disagreement among interpreters as to the symbolism of the colours and materials in the various curtains. This very disagreement speaks to the fact that it is very dangerous to impose symbolic meaning on the text which the Scripture does not give to it.'[2] Nevertheless, 'the covering of ram skins dyed red' seems to speak of atonement through the shedding of blood (Exod. 26:14; 36:19). Davis also discusses the difficulties of knowing the exact shape of the tabernacle but makes the point that its significance is more important than its actual shape.[3]

No beauty

'From a purely aesthetic point of view the tabernacle could not be considered a thing of beauty, at least from the outside. We might note that through the eyes of sinful men, Jesus Christ was also not seen in His real beauty (Isa. 53:2). When He tabernacled among men in flesh (John 1:14) He was rejected. The only ones who fully appreciated the beauty of the tabernacle were those who fellowshipped inside by means of blood atonement. So it is today. The only ones who fully appreciate and love the Christ ... are those who are of the royal priesthood of Christ and know Him as their personal Saviour.'[4]

God's pattern

God tells Moses how to erect the tabernacle and what to place inside it in Exodus 25-31, and in chapters 35-38 we read about the Israelites' obedience to these detailed instructions. Measurements for the tabernacle and the items inside are given in cubits. A cubit was the distance from the elbow to the tip of the fingers – a measurement of about 44 to 45 centimetres.

The Hebrews must follow God's pattern: 'Make this tabernacle and all its furnishings exactly like the pattern I will show you' (25:9,40; Heb. 8:5). Paul wrote to Timothy, 'What you heard from me, keep as the pattern of sound teaching, with faith and love in Christ Jesus' (2 Tim. 1:13). 'As Moses was to follow the pattern which God gave him on the mountain, so his people today are to follow the pattern of sound teaching which we read in the Bible. When a little child scribbles all over the page in his colouring book, instead of keeping to the printed pattern, he spoils the look of the whole thing. When believers fail to keep to the standards which God has laid down in the Bible they spoil their Christian witness, and bring the gospel into disrepute.'[5]

God's purpose

Why did God command Moses to set up a sanctuary? The tabernacle symbolised God's presence and served as a meeting place between God and his people: 'Make a sanctuary for me, and I will dwell among them'; 'There, above the cover between the two cherubim that are over the ark of the Testimony, I will meet with you and give you all my commands for the Israelites' (25:8,22). Moses placed the ark in the Holy of Holies where the high priest alone could enter once a year and only after the death of a sacrificial animal. Fellowship with God is through shed blood – then and now. We enjoy fellowship with God because Christ the Lamb died for us.

Willing offerings

God says to Moses, 'Tell the Israelites to bring me an offering. You are to receive the offering for me from each man whose heart prompts him to give' (Exod. 25:1-2). The mention of 'an offering' and the 'heart' indicate that this was an invitation rather than a direct command. Contributions for the erection of the tabernacle were completely voluntary. Moses addresses 'the Israelites' – nobody was excluded. No amount is specified, each one is left to give as his 'heart prompts him'. Verses 3-7 show that the Israelites' giving was costly. These gifts were not for Moses but 'for me' – the God who had delivered his people from Egyptian slavery. Both men and women brought their offerings following the example of their leaders (Exod. 35:22,27). The women freely used their weaving skills and 'the skilled craftsmen' willingly used their talents as an offering for the Lord (verses 25-26; 36:4). Everything was offered and the tabernacle erected as 'the LORD through Moses had commanded' (Exod. 35:29).

The Israelites were so enthusiastic that the craftsmen reported, 'The people are bringing more than enough', and Moses therefore restrained them from making further contributions. A similar spirit was shown in David's time when preparations for constructing the temple were undertaken (1 Chr. 29:1-3). How were these nomad Israelites able to donate these gifts? They left Egypt with 'articles of silver and gold and clothing' given by their neighbours (Exod. 3:22; 12:35-36) and may have purchased other materials from traders passing through the Sinai Peninsula.

The giving of Christians should exceed that of these Israelites because we serve the Lord Jesus Christ who 'was rich, yet for your sakes he became poor, so that you through his poverty might become rich' (2 Cor. 8:9). If we give ourselves completely to the Lord, then our giving will be generous, sacrificial and willing. God loves cheerful givers (2 Cor. 8:1-15; 9:6-7). Paul compares the church to a body in which every member has God-given gifts and ministries to use for the benefit of God's people (1 Cor. 12:1-31).

Christ at the centre

The Holy of Holies, containing the ark of the covenant, was the most important place in the tabernacle; everything else in the tent related to the events in that confined space on the annual Day of Atonement (Lev. 16). In front of the Holy of Holies was the Holy Place, an area curtained off from the wider tabernacle complex. The tabernacle had only one entrance situated on the east side of the courtyard (27:13-14) to teach us that Jesus is the only Saviour provided by God (John 14:6; Acts 4:12).

Moses erects the tabernacle at the centre of the Israelites' camp. 'The LORD said to Moses and to Aaron: "The Israelites are to camp around the Tent of Meeting some distance from it, each man under his own standard with the banners of his family"' (Num. 2:2). The 'Tent of Meeting' is another name for the tabernacle. 'The point is that God was to be the focal point, the very centre and heart of their lives, and his holiness translated into the reverence of keeping the appropriate distance – a constant reminder of their privilege and their need of redemption from sin.'[6] Our lives and our churches should focus on him. We should desire that 'in everything he might have the supremacy' (Col. 1:18).

It is now time to think about the various items within the tabernacle.

Outside the Holy Place

1. The *altar of burnt offering*, placed at the entrance, emphasized the holiness of God and the depravity of the sinner (Exod. 27:1-8; 38:1-7; Lev. 4:7,10,18). How may unworthy sinners approach the majestic God? Because of shed blood – for Jewish worshippers that meant an animal slain as a sacrifice; for believers this means Christ's blood offered on the altar of the cross. Atonement for sin demands a high price – the

taking of an innocent life. 'It was not a pleasant thing to see an innocent animal slaughtered and burned, but sin is an ugly thing and the sacrifice here, as well as that on Calvary, should be a vivid reminder of the hideousness of sin and its price.'[7]

'Offerings for sin were made continually upon this altar. This was because the people kept sinning again and again. Their sin offering only covered over the sin already committed and confessed; when they sinned again they had to make another offering.'[8] Hebrews 10 contrasts the daily sacrifices of the Jewish priests with the one sacrifice of Christ our great priest. He 'offered for all time one sacrifice for sins' (verse 12).

2. The priests washed in *the laver* before entering the Holy Place. The blood shed at the altar of burnt offering removes their guilt yet they still need washing. Likewise, believers freed from sin's guilt by Christ's death require washing. The altar speaks of once-for-all justification; the laver indicates ongoing sanctification. To put that another way – the altar represents what Christ has done *for* us; the laver represents what the Holy Spirit does *in* us. We wash as we apply God's Word in our lives (Ezek. 36:25-27; John 7:37-39; Eph. 5:25-27).

Inside the Holy Place

1. A table on which were placed twelve loaves of equal size – known as *the showbread* (Exod. 25:23-30; 37:10-16; Lev. 24:5-6). Each loaf represented one of the twelve tribes of Israel, whether the tribe was great or small. We see here a display of God's grace, treating all of his people equally. God does not choose us because of our merit but because of Christ's merits. The title 'bread of the Presence' signifies God's presence with his people (Exod. 25:30). As the bread fed the priests, so Jesus Christ, the bread of life, is food for our souls (John 6:25-59). We feed on him as we read his Word (Job 23:12; Psalm 119:103; 1 Peter 2:2-3). The bakers used the finest flour to make the

twelve loaves (Lev. 24:5-9) – Christ is the bread of the very finest flour; there is no imperfection in him.

2. *The lampstand* gave light to the priests in the Holy Place and pictures Christ as the light of the world (John 1:6-9; 8:12). Just as the gracious Saviour gave sight to the man born blind, so he gives sight to penitent sinners who are blinded from birth by Satan (John 9:1-41; 2 Cor. 4:4). Christ shines through the lives of individual Christians and through the corporate witness of his people (Matt. 5:14-16; Phil. 2:14-16). Moses made the lampstand of gold – perhaps to signify that Christ is the divine king – and kept it constantly alight by pure oil, a symbol of the Holy Spirit (Exod. 27:20-21).

The lampstand had six branches plus the central one making seven, the number that often speaks of completion, representing the entire church of God, throughout all history and drawn from all ethnic groups (Rev. 7:9). Christ's church is represented as a lampstand in Zechariah 4 and Revelation 1. Zechariah sees a seven-branched lampstand into which flows oil from two olive trees whereas John sees seven separate lampstands. The former signifies the unity of the universal church and the latter the independence of each local church. The two olive trees indicate the Holy Spirit who equips the church for her task of reflecting the character of God the Light in a dark world. We perform this task not by human strength but by God's power. The church cannot exhaust the oil of God's sustaining grace. The lampstand is gold to denote that the church is pure through Christ's blood, precious in God's sight and indestructible because of his power. John sees the risen Lord Jesus Christ, the prophet, priest and king, 'among the lampstands' (Rev. 1:13). He directs each church; he knows the successes and the sorrows of every church and of every member (Rev. 2-3).

3. *The altar of incense*, in front of the veil, (Exod. 30:1-10; 37:25-28) was the place where every morning and every evening Aaron burnt fragrant incense, a biblical symbol for

prayer (Ps. 141:2; Rev. 5:8, 8:3-4). The incense continuously burning – 'incense will burn regularly' (30:8) ('a perpetual incense', AV/NKJV) – reminds us of the necessity of persistent prayer (1 Thess. 5:17-18). God accepts our prayers because Christ is in heaven praying for us (Rom. 8:34; Heb. 7:22-28). He is our advocate before God's throne who speaks on our behalf (1 John 2:1-2).

4. *The curtain or veil* (Exod. 26:31-37; 36:35-38) formed a barrier to prevent access into the Holy of Holies into which the high priest alone entered on the yearly Day of Atonement. God tore down the veil from top to bottom when Christ, our great High Priest, bore our sins, once-for-all, on the cross (Mark 15:38; Heb. 10:19-25). The veil 'was woven of seventy twisted plaits, each plait consisting of twenty-four threads … It measured six feet by thirty and took three hundred priests to immerse it. That curtain was renewed annually, so this was no threadbare or frayed fabric that was suddenly torn in two.'[9]

Frederick Leahy helpfully explains the spiritual significance of the veil. 'It symbolized the flesh of Christ's humanity [Heb. 10:19-20] which in a sense concealed the most excellent glory of the Godhead. The Lord Jesus is the temple of God in perfection. He is Emmanuel, "God with us". Although few knew or understood, God dwelt amongst men in the person of Jesus the Nazarene (1. Tim. 1:16; John 1:14). In him "the whole fullness of deity dwells" (Col. 2:9). Yet there was concealment. It is significant that the veil of the supreme temple of Christ's body and the veil of that lesser temple were rent simultaneously … The "rent veil" indicated the end of the old Jewish religion … The Gospel door had been flung wide open.'[10]

In the Holy of Holies

The single item in the Holy of Holies was the ark of the covenant – the symbol of God's presence (Exod. 25:10-22;

37:1-9). The ark was a small box, measuring about 1.1 metres long by 70 centimetres wide and 70 centimetres high, made of acacia wood, overlaid with pure gold, both inside and out. What was inside the ark? Aaron's rod, a pot of manna and the stone tablets inscribed with the Ten Commandments (Heb. 9:4). The rod reminded the Israelites of their rebellion, the manna of the Lord's provision and the Ten Commandments of God's demand for obedience (Num. 17:1-12; Exod. 16:1-36; Exod. 20:1-21).

'Above the ark were the cherubim of the Glory, overshadowing the atonement cover' ('mercy seat', AV/ NKJV) (Heb. 9:5). The cherubim are angels that are distinct from the seraphim (Isa. 6:2). 'The cherubim apparently have to do with the holiness of God as violated by sin; the seraphim with uncleanness in the people of God.'[11] The cherubim, made of hammered gold, faced each other with wings outspread covering the ark, and looked down towards the ark. 'God placed cherubim at the east side of the Garden of Eden "to guard the way to the tree of life" (Gen. 3:24). The posture of the cherubim on the cover of the ark projects the idea of guarding the way to God.'[12] 'The Glory' (Heb. 9:5) refers to 'the radiant presence of God dwelling in the midst of His people'[13] – the Shekinah Glory that appeared above the tabernacle once it was erected (Exod. 25:22; Exod. 40:34-35).

The lid of the ark was the mercy seat on which the priest poured blood from a basin on the Day of Atonement (Exod. 25:17; Heb. 9:5,7). The blood proved that the sacrificial lamb had died instead of the guilty people. Christ is our 'mercy seat', whose blood covers our transgressions from God's holy sight. 'He went through the greater and more perfect tabernacle that is not man-made, that is to say, not a part of this creation. He did not enter by means of the blood of goats and calves; but he entered the Most Holy Place once for all by his own blood, having obtained eternal redemption.' Christ entered heaven having 'obtained eternal redemption' for believers who will live for ever with him (Heb. 9:11-12,24).

Paul picks up the 'mercy-seat' theme in Romans 3:25, 'God presented him as a sacrifice of atonement, through faith in his blood.' The AV translates 'sacrifice of atonement' as 'propitiation', defined in the NIV footnote as 'the one who would turn aside his wrath, taking away sin'. 'The Greek word ... indicates the blood-sprinkled lid of the ark of the covenant. This is the mercy seat', comments William Hendriksen.[14] God's wrath fell on Christ, our mercy seat, instead of falling on us!

After the tabernacle

Many years after Moses erected the tabernacle, Solomon, Israel's third king, built the magnificent temple in Jerusalem, which was destroyed by the invading armies of Nebuchadnezzar from 586 BC onwards. The exiles who returned to Jerusalem under the leadership of Zerubbabel in 538 BC rebuilt the temple over a period of twenty-one years, completing the restoration about seventy years after its destruction (Ezra 1-6).[15] Antiochus Epiphanes, one of the Syrian kings who ruled Palestine, desecrated the second temple in 167 BC. In 37 BC, Herod the Great became King of the Jews and built a temple that the Romans destroyed in AD 70. God's temple is now the church – believers – in which he lives by his Holy Spirit: 'We are the temple of the living God. As God has said: "I will live with them and walk among them, and I will be their God, and they will be my people."' (2 Cor. 6:16). Jesus taught that our attitude when we worship is more important than where we worship. God looks for a sincere heart rather than elaborate ritual (John 4:19-24).

The tabernacle of God

As John nears the end of his life, he sees 'a new heaven and a new earth'. He sees Christ's church – 'the Holy City, the new Jerusalem ... a bride beautifully dressed for her husband' –

coming from heaven to live on the new earth. The apostle hears Christ's voice saying, 'Now the dwelling of God is with men, and he will live with them. They will be his people, and God himself will be with them and be their God' (Rev 21:1-3). The AV/NKJV translates 'dwelling of God' in verse 3 as 'the tabernacle of God' – this is a reference to the tabernacle in the wilderness. In Revelation 21, the Holy City and the tabernacle become one. 'God's abode shall be with men perfectly and completely. We shall be like Him. And God shall dwell in all of us perfectly. He will fill us, enlighten us, quicken our love, bind us to Himself with unbreakable bonds of everlasting friendship. And we shall know Him and love Him and serve Him and taste His goodness to the full.'[16]

13.
Christix the great High Priest
——————— (Exod. 28-29) ———————

Aaron, Israel's first high priest, and the garments he wore when performing his duties teach us about the Lord Jesus Christ, our great high priest in heaven. We look at Aaron's ephod, breastplate, robe and turban besides the clothes worn by the other priests. The high priest entered the Holy of Holies once a year on the Day of Atonement, wearing precious stones on his shoulders and near his heart, representing the twelve tribes of Israel. Christ represents believers in heaven; each one is precious to him. All believers are now priests who present their bodies as living sacrifices to God (Rom. 12:1).

'Aaron and his sons shall serve me as priests, and this is what they shall wear', says God to Moses in Exodus 28. Exodus 39 records Moses' obedience to this command. 'This is how you are to consecrate Aaron as high priest' says God in Exodus 29. Leviticus 8 informs us that Moses did exactly as God said.

Why should 21st century Christians examine the wardrobe of an ancient Hebrew priest? Because Aaron, Moses' brother, is a type of the Lord Jesus Christ, our great High Priest. As we saw in chapter 1, 'types are persons, or objects or events that serve as prophetic illustrations or likenesses of New Testament fulfilments.'[1] The writer to the Hebrews develops the theme of

Christ our great High Priest, and puts in our hands the key to unlock Exodus 28 (see especially Heb. 4:14-16; 10:1-39).

The high priest went once a year into the Holy of Holies to atone for the sins of the nation. The other priests assisted the high priest but had no importance apart from his ministry, just as the daily sacrifices related to the annual Day of Atonement and had no significance apart from that yearly offering and its ritual. The priests bringing the daily sacrifices and the high priest presenting to God the yearly offering were signposts to Jesus Christ, whose death accomplished what the old sacrifices could never achieve. 'It is impossible for the blood of bulls and goats to take away sins ... But when this priest [Christ] had offered for all time one sacrifice for sins, he sat down at the right hand of God' (Heb. 10: 4,12).

We read in Exodus 28 about the garments worn by Aaron and all the high priests after him, who must come from the tribe of Levi and specifically from the family of Aaron (verses 6-38), and then we read about the vestments for the common priests (verses 39-43).

God tells Moses to instruct 'skilled men ... to make garments for Aaron ... These are the garments they are to make: a breastpiece, an ephod, a robe, a woven tunic, a turban and a sash ... Make them use gold, and blue, purple and scarlet yarn, and fine linen' (verses 3-5).[2]

The ephod (28:6-14)

The ephod was a lovely two-piece sleeveless apron or waistcoat, held to the body by an ornamental belt and joined at the shoulders by straps. The straps had two onyx stones ('a kind of quartz with alternating coloured layers, used as a gemstone'[3]) bearing the names of the twelve tribes of Israel, six on each stone.

These stones were 'memorial stones for the sons of Israel' (verse 12) because the Israelites were in the thoughts of the high priest whenever he appeared before the Lord. Christ our High

Priest perpetually remembers us in heaven. He prays for us when we are tempted and sympathises with us when we suffer (Rom. 8:33-34; Heb 2:18, 4:14-16, 7:25). Unlike the Jewish priest, the divine priest does not need sleep and will never die, nor does he suffer from a failing memory. He does not finish his shift and hand over his duties to another priest; he personally and constantly remembers every one of his elect by name.

Aaron bore the names of Israel's twelve tribes on his two shoulders to indicate that the high priest was the helper of God's people (Exod. 28:12). However, Jewish priests came 'from among men' and were therefore 'subject to weakness' (Heb. 5:1-2), whereas Christ, our High Priest exalted in heaven, is strong enough to meet our every need; he is the almighty God!

The breastplate (28:15-30)

The breastplate consisted of a square piece of beautiful material folded in half with an opening at the top like a pouch, placed over the front of the ephod and adorned with twelve precious stones set in gold and arranged in four rows of three. Each of these stones had the name of an Israelite tribe engraved on it. The precise identification of some of these precious stones is uncertain.

When 'the high priest went into the presence of God he carried with him the names of all the Israelites, in two places. He bore their names on his shoulders; this indicated the responsibilities of the high priest to care for them. And he carried them on his heart; this was to show the love which he had for them.'[4]

What is the difference between the stones on the ephod and those on the breastplate? The ephod had two stones for all twelve tribes; on the breastplate, each tribe had its own stone. The priest represented each tribe individually when he entered the Holy of Holies. He took each tribe by name into God's presence. Christ prays for each one of his people and presents their personal needs to his Father. We are always on the heart and in the thoughts of our great High Priest. We are his precious jewels (Mal. 3:17, AV).

Aaron acted specifically as the high priest for the nation of Israel. God chose this nation to be his own people, so that from that race he might bring into the world the Lord Jesus Christ. The church is now 'a chosen people, a royal priesthood, a holy nation, a people belonging to God' (1 Peter 2:9). Christ is the great High Priest, not of the world, but of his church purchased with his blood (1 Peter 1:18-19; Eph. 5:25-27). Jesus prayed on the eve of his death, 'I am not praying for the world, but for those you have given me, for they are yours' (John 17:9).

The breastplate had two special stones known as 'the Urim and the Thummim ... the means of making decisions for the Israelites', hence the description, 'a breastpiece for making decisions' (Exod. 28:15,30). The exact nature of the 'Urim and Thummim' is unknown.[5] Bentley comments, 'One stone appears to have symbolised curses, and the other perfections ... No one today knows how they were used to discover the will of God for his people, but Proverbs 16:33 may give us a clue. There we read, "The lot is cast into the lap, but its every decision is from the Lord."'[6] The stones showed that God gave to the priest the authority to ask him for directions on behalf of the nation.

The words 'Urim and Thummim' mean 'lights and perfections'; we have a reliable light to guide us in this dark world – the inerrant Scriptures written by holy men of God who spoke as they were moved by the Holy Spirit (2 Peter 1:19-21). The Christian echoes the words of the Psalmist, 'Your word is a lamp to my feet and a light for my path' (Ps. 119:105). Our great High Priest guides us by his Word.

The robe (28:31-35)

The high priest wore a sleeveless blue robe under the ephod, similar to a Mexican poncho, which reached a little below the knees with bells and pomegranates on its hem. The ringing bells assured the worshippers that the priest hidden from view in the Holy Place and in the inner shrine of the Holy of Holies was still alive! The tinkling bell 'as the priest left the tabernacle called for great rejoicing for the atonement had been completed' and accepted by the holy God.[7] Christ replaces our rags of sin with his spotless robe of righteousness so that we may go boldly, by prayer, into God's presence (Isa. 64:6, 61:10; Heb 4:16).

What may we learn from the 'pomegranates of blue, purple and scarlet yarn around the hem of the robe'? (verse 33). Henry Law, a 19th century evangelical Anglican, puts forward the idea that because the pomegranate is a fruit 'rich in seed' it represents the success of Christ's death. His seed – those for whom he died – will be numerous. 'Mark the crowds who throng the throne of glory. They are all the product of redeeming love'[8] (Isa. 53:10-11; Rev. 7:9).

The turban (28:36-38)

The priest wore on his turban a gold plate bearing the words 'HOLY TO THE LORD' (verse 36). The word 'holy' 'signifies that Aaron has been especially set apart to his task as high priest. As a representative of Israel, he may also reflect Israel's status of being set apart from all other peoples on the earth.'[9] God commands Moses to consecrate Aaron, and his sons, 'so that they may serve *me*' (verses 1,3-4; emphasis added).

Why was Aaron set apart? To 'bear the guilt ... so that they [the Israelites] will be acceptable to the LORD' (verse 38). 'The high priest, as the representative of all Israel, will incur responsibility for the sins of Israel and then make sacrificial atonement for them.'[10] Christ took responsibility for our sins. He was treated by God as the sinner to give us acceptance with God. 'God made him who had no sin to be sin for us, so that in him we might become the righteousness of God' (2 Cor. 5:21). God set us apart from before time to bring glory to himself by holy living (Eph. 1:4-6). We should frequently ask ourselves, 'Are my thoughts, attitudes, desires, words and actions holy to the Lord?'

The priest's clothes (28:39-43)

Besides wearing 'the tunic', the 'turban of fine linen' and 'the sash' ('some kind of girdle to be worn over the tunic and under the robe'[11]), the priests wore 'linen undergarments' to cover their bodies. They were white to signify purity; only the pure can enter God's presence. However, no one is pure enough, not even the Jewish priest who had 'to offer sacrifices for his own sins as well as for those of the people' (Heb. 5:3). Therefore, Moses washed Aaron and his four sons at the entrance of the Tent of Meeting (the tabernacle) before dressing them in the vestments because the priest must be physically and spiritually clean for his work (29:4-5). Sin-offerings were made to atone for the sins of the priests and the people, every day for seven days (29:10-26,35-37). Christians come to God through Christ, the only sinless Priest whose blood washes their souls clean from all sin (1 John 1:7,9).

We read in Exodus 29:7 about the anointing of the priest. 'Take the anointing oil and anoint him by pouring it on his head.' The Holy Spirit came like a dove and anointed Jesus at his baptism. Shortly after this event, Jesus entered the synagogue in Nazareth and read from Isaiah 61: 'The Spirit of the Lord is on me, because he has anointed me to preach good news to the poor.' He then declared, 'Today this scripture is fulfilled in your hearing.' Following his ascension into heaven, Christ poured out the Holy Spirit on his church 'to preach the good news' (Luke 3:21-22, 4:16-21; John 15:26-27; Acts 1:4-5,8).

Spiritual priests

The priests' garments gave Aaron and his sons 'dignity and honour' (verses 2,40; 'glory and beauty', AV/NKJV). 'The priestly office was intentionally elevated in the eyes of the people. This apparel would serve to distinguish the priests as a class by themselves and in a certain sense above the rest of the nation. The distinctiveness of the garments along with their beauty would be a constant reminder to the priests themselves of their holy station [office] and its demand for consecrated living ... These sacred garments were always to be worn when the priests served in the sanctuary but never at other times.'[12]

The priesthood is no longer restricted to an elite group within the church; now all believers, male and female, are priests who bring to the great High Priest the offering of their lives, their praise and their service (Heb. 13:15-16; 1 Peter 2:5,9). The whole of life, every day of every week throughout the year, is spiritual worship offered to God: 'I urge you ... to offer your bodies as living sacrifices, holy and pleasing to God – this is your spiritual act of worship' (Rom. 12:1).

Perhaps we have an anticipation of Romans 12:1 in Exodus 29:20, where we read that God commands Moses to put animal blood on 'the lobes of the right ears of Aaron and his sons, on the thumbs of their right hands, and on the big toes of their right feet'. What is the significance of this ritual? Ears represent obedience; we listen to obey. Hands and toes represent service; we are ready to go wherever God sends and do whatever he commands.

14.

Christ the Mediator

───── (Exod. 32) ─────

Moses, the mediator of the old covenant, earnestly prays twice for God to spare Israel after the incident of the golden calf. Moses boldly presents reasons to God why he should not destroy the people whom he has chosen and delivered from Egypt. Moses refuses God's offer to make his descendants into a great nation. He even asks God to deprive him of eternal life, if only he will pardon his sinful people. God rejects Moses' proposal. However, Christ the Mediator of the new covenant dies to appease God's wrath. God pardons our sins because of Christ's death and because of Christ's intercession for us in heaven.

Do you ever feel uneasy about the actions of God? Do you find it hard to understand his activities? For example, God says to Moses, 'Now leave me alone so that my anger may burn against them and that I may destroy them' (Exod. 32:10). God threatened to destroy his chosen people after delivering them from slavery in Egypt and caring for them in the inhospitable desert. A few verses later we read that 'the LORD relented and did not bring on his people the disaster he had threatened' (verse 14). Does the Lord change his mind so quickly? Was he now getting over his bad mood? God, whose wisdom is perfect, does not need to change his plans. Neither does the unchanging God have mood swings, one moment loving and the next malicious. However, God's attitude towards us may change: if we obey him, like Moses, we enjoy his favour, when we disobey him, like the Israelites, he is angry with us.

Between God's warning of punishment and his rescinding that threat in Exodus 32, Moses implores the just God to spare his special people, 'Turn from your fierce anger; relent and do not bring disaster on your people' (verse 12). It was God's plan that he would show mercy to Israel because of Moses' prayer to teach us about Christ the Mediator who pleads with God to save sinners from his eternal anger. We must not think of the loving Son persuading an irate Father to pardon transgressors. God's love motivated him to give his precious Son to save sinners (John 3:16; 1 John 4:10).

Israel's sin

Can you remember an occasion when you heard a stirring sermon that made you determined to live closer to God? How long was it before your resolve gave way when faced with powerful temptation? The Israelites behaved in the same way in the wilderness. 'We will do everything the LORD has said; we will obey', chorused God's people when Moses read 'the Book of the Covenant', containing the moral law – the Ten Commandments – and other laws relating specifically to Israel (Exod. 24:7). Only a few weeks later the Israelites bow down to a golden calf; this was 'one of the dark moments in Israel's history'[1] (Exod. 32). Therefore, God says to Moses 'Now leave me alone so that my anger may burn against them and that I may destroy them' (verse 10).

Why was God so angry with his people when they worshipped the golden calf? They had wilfully broken the first and second commandments: 'You shall have no other gods before me. You shall not make for yourself an idol in the form of anything in heaven above or on the earth beneath or in the waters below. You shall not bow down to them or worship them' (Exod. 20:3-5). They had also broken the third commandment, 'You shall not misuse the name of the LORD your God' when they attributed their release from oppression to the golden calf and celebrated 'a festival to the LORD' before the image (32:4-5). The words 'indulge in revelry' in verse 6 and the words 'running wild' and 'out of control' in verse 25 suggest immorality and therefore a breach of the seventh commandment, 'you shall not commit adultery' (Exod. 20:14). The seventh commandment includes all sexual deviations. Paul refers to this event in 1 Corinthians 10:7, 'Do not be idolaters, as some of them were; as it is written: "The people sat down to eat and drink and got up to indulge in pagan revelry."' The AV/NKJV translates 'pagan revelry' as 'play', 'a euphemism for sexual relations. It means sexual play and is the same word translated as "caressing" in Gen. 26:8.'[2] Young bulls were regarded as symbols of fertility.

Moses breaking 'the two tablets' symbolised the nation's breaking God's laws (Exod. 32:19). They had not merely broken human laws but those inscribed by God himself (verses 15-16). Burning the golden calf and making the people drink water into which the ashes had been scattered showed the uselessness of man-made gods (verses 20). Moses 'was so furious with them that in a sense he made them drink their own religion.'[3]

Why should Israel obey God? Because he redeemed his people from bondage: 'I am the LORD your God, who brought you out of Egypt, out of the land of slavery' (Exod. 20:2). The Israelites were also to obey God because he was like a husband to Israel his wife. This is why he declares, 'I, the LORD your God, am a jealous God' (verse 5). He punishes the disobedient and shows mercy to the obedient (verses 5-6). The word 'LORD' (Jehovah/Yahweh) in Exodus 20:4-5 looks back to Christ's appearance to Moses in the burning bush, when he called him to lead the Hebrews from captivity to freedom (Exod. 3).[4]

The Israelites deserved punishment because they broke God's law although they had seen God's awesome power displayed in the plagues and in the dramatic crossing of the Red Sea. Besides this, they experienced God's love in the daily provision of the manna, quails and water from the rock. Furthermore, God sent a cloud by day and a pillar of fire by night to defend the Israelites, and bore patiently with their constant grumbling against him. What more could God do for his people?

How does God view his people's sin? He says they 'have become corrupt' and 'they are a stiff-necked people' (Exod. 32:7,9). He means corrupt like a rotting piece of meat and self-willed 'like an ox or horse which refuses to respond when its master pulls its rope or harness, to lead it to work'.[5] 'They have been quick to turn away from what I commanded' is God's charge against them (verse 8). God disowns them – they are '*your* people' he tells Moses (verse 7). No Israelite could dispute that punishment was richly deserved.

We too deserve God's wrath. We are born as sinners and even as children, we deliberately break God's law (Ps. 51:5; Isa. 53:6; 1 John 3:4). We become Christians through a new birth but still we sin against our Redeemer and prove unfaithful to our divine Husband. Like Israel, we sometimes despise God's power, do not value his love and often test his patience. What hope is there for us? There is hope because Christ the Mediator came from heaven to live a perfect life as our representative, thus fulfilling the demands of God's law for us. God pours his wrath on his own beloved Son when he died on the cross: 'Christ redeemed us from the curse of the law by becoming a curse for us' (Gal. 3:13). The sinner was under the curse, but Christ took up a position between the sinner and the curse so that the curse came upon him. God acquits us because he condemns the Mediator in our place.

When we read Exodus 32 alongside Romans 1:18-32 and Romans 3:9-18 we see that sins similar to Israel's are characteristics of a fallen nature; these passages give us a sad, but realistic portrait of human degeneracy and the urgent need of a sinless Mediator. We ought to thank God for his restraining grace that keeps us from the depths of depravity into which others fall!

Aaron's weakness

Moses' six weeks' absence from the camp prompts the Israelites to ask Aaron to 'make us gods who will go before us', and to deride the God-appointed leader: 'As for this fellow Moses who brought us up out of Egypt, we don't know what has happened to him' (Exod. 32:1-2). Though the original suggestion came from the people, Moses, speaking on behalf of God, holds Aaron responsible for their actions, '*you* led them into such great sin' (verses 1,21). Aaron proves a weak leader in a crisis. He fears men more than he fears God. Aaron, the man who spoke as God's mouthpiece (4:10-17; 7:1-2), makes a pathetic excuse for his conduct: 'They gave me the gold, and I threw it into the fire, and out came this calf' (verse 24). The plural 'gods' (verses 1,4,8) may mean that the calf was seen as being in partnership with God and so Aaron proclaims 'a festival to the LORD' in front of the golden calf (verse 5).

Making a golden calf showed that the Israelites' hearts were still in Egypt because they copied the Egyptians who worshipped a bull-shaped god named Apis. They chose a calf, the symbol of a strong and fertile animal, because they wanted a strong god to lead them to a new and fertile home.

Moses' first prayer

Moses first prayer (Exod. 32:11-14) follows God's offer, 'I will make you into a great nation' (verse 10). Moses, 'a very humble man, more humble than anyone else on the face of the earth' (Num. 12:3), ignores this offer because of his concern for Israel. God's glory is more important to him than his own. Moses' selfless attitude foreshadows Christ's attitude before his incarnation. 'Christ Jesus ... being in very nature

God, did not consider equality with God something to be grasped, but made himself nothing, taking the very nature of a servant, being made in human likeness.' He is still God but how different is his life on earth to that he enjoyed in heaven! The sovereign Lord becomes a servant! He looked not to his own interests but to the interests of his people. We are to copy his humility (Phil. 2:4-8).

How does Moses pray for Israel facing execution? Moses, who rejected acclaim for himself, ardently defended God's glory. Moses uses three arguments in Exodus 32. Firstly, the Israelites belong to God; they are 'your people' (verse 11). Secondly, Moses imagines the Egyptians deriding God if he destroyed Israel: 'God is cruel; he took the Hebrews into the desert to massacre them' (verses 11-12). Thirdly, Moses reminds God of his promises to the patriarchs of 'descendants as numerous as the stars in the sky' living in a land given to them as 'their inheritance forever' (verse 13). The promises made to Abraham, Isaac and Jacob look beyond the Jewish race to Christ, the Saviour of the world, and the salvation of his universal church (see Gal. 3). The redeemed in heaven will be too many to count (Rev. 7:9-11).

Currid argues that 'relent' ('repented', AV) in verse 14 would be better translated as 'compassion'; God's judgement 'was tempered by mercy' because of Moses' prayer.[6] God did not wipe Israel 'off the face of the earth' (verse 12), nevertheless, he calls on the Levites, who declared themselves 'for the LORD' to punish the unrepentant – among them some of their own families. We read that 'about three thousand of the people died' (verses 26-29). God struck those who remained with a plague (verse 35). We must take God's holiness and his honour seriously.

Moses' command, 'Whoever is for the LORD, come to me' (verse 26) has an echo in Jesus' call to discipleship. 'If anyone comes to me and does not hate his father and mother, his wife and children, his brothers and sisters – yes, even his own life – he cannot be my disciple. And anyone who does not carry his cross and follow me cannot be my disciple' (Luke 14:26-27). What is the meaning of the word 'hate'? If we are to love even our enemies, should we not love our family? This is surely demanded in the commandment to 'honour your father and your mother' (Matt. 5:43-48; Exod. 20:12). 'The word "hate" means to love less ... What the Saviour demands ... is complete devotion, the type of loyalty that is so true and unswerving that every other attachment, even that to one's wife, must be subjected to it.'[7] We see an illustration of this 'complete devotion' in the Levites, who loved God more than they loved their disobedient family members.

Moses' second prayer

On 'the next day', Moses prays a second time (verses 30-32). Israel's 'great sin' needs atonement, but the blood of animals could not effectively remove sin; therefore Moses offers himself as a sacrifice to God, 'Please forgive their sin – but if not, then blot me out of the book you have written' (verse 32).[8] God does not accept this offer because Moses himself is a sinner and just as each person must bear the responsibility for his own sin, so must the nation: 'When the time comes for me to punish, I will punish them for their sins' (verses 33-34). God's time to punish the rebellious nation came at 'length, when the stiff-necked people had filled up the measure of their sin through repeated rebellion against Jehovah and His servant Moses, and were sentenced at Kadesh to die out in the wilderness'[9] (Num. 14:26-45). Meanwhile, Moses, guided by God's angel, will lead his people towards the promised land (Exod. 32:34). 'My angel' is probably 'the Angel of the LORD', Jesus Christ, who appeared to Moses at the burning bush (Exod. 3:2).[10]

'Moses himself had done no wrong, yet, because he loved these wicked people so much, he even said that he was prepared for the Lord to expunge his own name from God's book. In the New Testament this is called "the Lamb's book of Life" (Rev. 21: 27). Moses, who was the mediator between God and the

Israelites, offered to die in their place. What a powerful picture this verse [32] is of the Lord Jesus! He actually did die on the cross to pay the price of the sins of his people.'[11]

Repentance

God tells his people, 'Go up to the land flowing with milk and honey. But I will not go up with you, because you are a stiff-necked people and I might destroy you on the way.' How do they respond to this distressing news? 'They began to mourn' and as evidence of their penitence they 'stripped off their ornaments at Mount Horeb' (Exod. 33:1-6). 'Putting off their ornaments was an outward demonstration of the fact that they realised that in making and worshipping the golden calf they had sinned greatly. They knew that they needed to do something to demonstrate to God, and to each other, that they truly repented of their sinful actions.'[12] We must allow nothing to come between us and our dedication to God.

Why do we read about worshipping the golden calf between the instructions for the erection of the tabernacle? To teach us that repentance comes before worship. Penitence is the path to the Lord Jesus Christ, the Mediator in heaven.

15.

Christ the Shekinah glory
—— (Exod. 24, 33, 34 and 40) ——

Christ revealed himself to Moses and the Israelites as 'the pillar of cloud' – 'the glory of the LORD' – that hovered over Mount Sinai and later rested over the tabernacle. We look at the passages where we read about Christ, the Shekinah glory – Exod. 24, 33, 34 and 40 – and place these alongside NT texts such as 1 Cor. 13:12 and 2 Cor. 3.

'You cannot see my face, for no-one may see me and live' – this is God's reply to Moses' request, 'Now show me your glory.' God's answer appears to contradict a statement we read earlier in the same chapter: 'The LORD would speak to Moses face to face, as a man speaks with his friend' (Exod. 33:11,18,20). Back in chapter 24, we read that Moses, Aaron, his two sons and the seventy elders 'saw God, and they ate and drank' (verses 9-11). They saw God but did *not* die; they felt joy rather than fear in God's holy presence. How do we explain this apparent contradiction?

We cannot see God because 'God is spirit' which means that he has no physical body (John 4:24). According to the apostle Paul, he is 'the King eternal, immortal, invisible, the only God' who 'lives in unapproachable light, whom no-one has seen or can see' (1 Tim. 1:17; 6:16). Why then do we read in the Scriptures about God having physical features such as a face, eyes, ears and hands?[1] The biblical writers want us to understand the character of the invisible God; they are describing how he deals with and reacts to sinners, besides his care of believers, rather than depicting his physical appearance. Furthermore, we cannot see God's face and live because God's eyes 'are too pure to look on evil; [he] cannot tolerate wrong' (Hab. 1:13). One look at God and we would shrivel up like hay in a fire.

How then could Moses and the Israelite leaders see God and not die? How could God speak 'face to face' with Moses? They saw Christ who revealed himself as 'the pillar of cloud' – 'the glory of the LORD' – the cloud of fire hovering over Mount Sinai (24:15-17), visible at the entrance of the tent of meeting pitched outside the camp (33:7-11), descending when Moses chiselled the two tablets of stone (34:4-5) and filling the tabernacle (40:34-38). Moses caught a glimpse of the Lord's glory (33:21-23) and reflected this glory in his face after he had been alone with God on Mount Sinai (34:29-35). To quote Currid's comments on Exodus 14:19-20, 'The pillar of cloud … moved to stand between Israel and Egypt. This is the theophany of Yahweh [Jehovah] that leads Israel out of Egypt into the wilderness (13:21-22). It is the Shekinah glory by which God often makes his presence known to his people (19:9; 33:9-10).'[2] 'Shekinah' is 'a transliteration of a Hebrew word not found in the Bible but used in many of the Jewish writings to speak of God's presence. The term means "that which dwells".'[3]

Let's now look at the passages in Exodus, where we read about 'the glory of the LORD' – Christ, the Shekinah glory.

Moses sees God (Exod. 24)

The events of Exodus 24 took place after God gave Moses the Ten Commandments. He also gave Moses laws relating to Israel's life in the wilderness, besides giving him commands to prepare the Hebrews for their future in the promised land. Moses reads these laws to the people and writes them in a book known as 'the book of the Covenant'. The Israelites 'responded with one voice, "Everything the LORD has said we will do"' (verse 3). Moses builds an altar, sends young men to offer calves to the Lord, and then sprinkles some of the animal's blood on the altar (verses 3-6). After a further reading, the people repeat their promise to obey God, and then Moses sprinkles some of the blood on them saying, 'This is the blood of the covenant that the LORD has made with you in accordance with all these words' (verses 7-8).

The blood of these young bulls pointed forward to Christ, God's Lamb, who died once-for-all, to take away the sin of the world (John 1:29; cf. Heb. 10:1-18). 'The blood of the covenant' (Exod. 24:8) directs us to Christ's words on the evening of his death: 'This cup is [represents] the new covenant in my blood, which is poured out for you.' At Calvary, Christ shed 'the blood of the eternal covenant' (Luke 22:20; Heb. 13:20-21). His blood signed the covenant. Christ made a solemn promise to save God's elect; the believer, once saved, makes a solemn promise to obey God. It is through Christ's blood that we draw near to God (Heb. 10:19-20).

So we come to the verses already referred to, where we read that 'Moses and Aaron, Nadab and Abihu, and the seventy elders ... saw the God of Israel ... but God did not raise his hand against these leaders' (Exod. 24:9-11). 'What they perceived was certainly a theophany ... It is similar to the descriptions of the throne-settings in the visions of Isaiah and Ezekiel (Isa. 6:1-8; Ezek 1:22).'[4] Why did God not destroy Moses and his companions? Because atoning blood had been shed and because they saw Christ – God the Son, rather than God the Father. As they looked at God, they saw that 'under his feet was something like a pavement made of sapphire, [lapis-lazuli] clear as the sky itself.' Currid translates 'as heaven for clarity' and comments 'it was as if heaven had partially descended to earth.' He also suggests that the word 'clear' or 'clarity' may indicate 'purity and moral cleanness'.[5] Having seen God, 'they ate and drank', expressing their fellowship with God (verse 11).

Now God calls Moses and Joshua to leave the elders and go further up the mountain. Later, Moses leaves even Joshua his trusted aide, and disappears into the cloud surrounding Mount Sinai, where he stayed 'forty days and forty nights' (verses 12-18). During this time, God gave Moses instructions for building the tabernacle, and the other information that we find in the next six chapters of Exodus. Jesus also spent forty days and forty nights in the desert without eating or drinking, alone with God his Father. His first temptation arose from his hunger after this long fast (Matt. 4:1-4).

To the Israelites 'the glory of the LORD looked like a consuming fire on top of the mountain' (Exod. 24:17). They were struck with fear that the fire would burn them; this terror is rather surprising after eating and drinking in God's presence. The writer to the Hebrews describes God as 'a consuming fire' and Peter predicts the day when Christ will come and the present world 'will be destroyed by fire'. However, out of the ashes of the burning world will arise 'a new heaven and a new earth, the home of righteousness' (Heb. 12:29; 2 Peter 3:10-13). God's wrath will burn up the rubbish of sin. However, because Christ bore God's wrath for us, we, like Moses, enjoy fellowship with God now, and will enter his presence later – not just for forty days and forty nights, but for ever.

Moses desires God's presence (Exod. 33)

Following the incident of the golden calf[6], Moses pitched a tent 'outside the camp some distance away, calling it the "tent of meeting"'. Once inside the tent, 'the pillar of cloud would come down and stay at the entrance, while the LORD spoke with Moses.' In this tent, 'The LORD would speak to Moses face to face, as a man speaks with his friend.' We read that the people 'stood and worshipped, each at the entrance to his tent' (Exod. 33: 7-11). This 'tent of meeting' was not the tabernacle which Moses had not yet erected, though this title was later given to that structure (Exod. 40:34). The holy God separates himself from his sinful people by speaking to Moses 'outside the camp'.

The expression 'face to face' in Exodus 33:11 means 'mouth to mouth' and indicates that God spoke to Moses just like someone talking to a close friend. The words suggest a physical appearance of God as in Exodus 24:9-10: 'Moses … *saw* the God of Israel.'

This interpretation of Exodus 33:11 finds support in Numbers 12:6-8 where we read God's rebuke of Miriam and Aaron when they criticised Moses. 'When a prophet of the LORD is among you, I reveal myself to him in visions, I speak to him in dreams. But this is not true of my servant Moses; he is faithful in all my house.[7] With him I speak face to face, clearly and not in riddles; he sees the form of the LORD. Why then were you not afraid to speak against my servant Moses?' Moses saw the invisible God in some kind of physical form. Surely 'the form of the LORD' was the pre-incarnate Christ.[8] Moses saw God because he saw Christ; this makes Moses unique among the prophets.

Contrasting the Christian's present understanding and his future understanding, the apostle Paul writes, 'Now we see but a poor reflection as in a mirror; then we shall see face to face. Now I know in part; then I shall know fully even as I am fully known' (1 Cor. 13:12; cf. 1 John 3:2).[9] What we now know, though true, is imperfect and incomplete. One day we will have perfect knowledge and enjoy unhindered and eternal fellowship with God.

Moses, as the mediator of God's people, prays for God rather than an angel, (Exod. 33:2) – in contrast to 'my angel' ['the Angel of the LORD', i.e. Christ] (Exod. 23:23) – to go with them as they leave Sinai and travel to Canaan. The prayer for God's presence is based on God's special favour to himself – 'I know you by name and you have favour with me' – and God's relationship to the Israelites – 'your people' (Exod. 33:12-13). God had called the Israelites 'the people' (verse 1) and 'these people' (verse 12) but now Moses boldly declares, 'Remember that this nation is *your* people' (verse 13, emphasis added). He dares to remind the almighty God of his responsibility for his own people. Then Moses suggests that God must show to the surrounding nations that he was pleased with his chosen people and their human leader (verse 16).

How does God respond to Moses? He gives his servant a delightful promise: 'My Presence will go with you, and I will give you rest' (verse 14). 'Presence' in the Hebrew is 'face', and looks back to God speaking 'face to face' with Moses (verse 11). 'The "face" of Jehovah is Jehovah in His own personal presence, and is identical with the "angel" in whom the name of Jehovah was (Exod. 23:20-21), and who is therefore called in Isaiah 63:9 "the angel of His face" ['presence', NIV].'[10] The Angel who has God's Name in him is 'the Angel of the LORD' who appeared to Moses at the burning bush – he is Christ.[11]

The term 'rest' used by God in Exodus 33:14 often refers to the possession of the promised land (Deut. 3:20; 12:10). God's promise in Exodus 33:14 finds an echo in Jesus' promise in Matthew 11:28, 'Come to me, all you who are weary and burdened, and I will give you rest', and in his parting words in Matthew 28:20, 'I am with you always, to the very end of the age.' Christ gives rest from trying to earn salvation. His death opens the door into the eternal rest of heaven.

Encouraged by God's promise of his Presence, Moses prays 'Now show me your glory' (Exod. 33:18). He is praying to see God's essential glory – what makes God who he is – which no one can see and live (verse 20). Nevertheless, God graciously answers Moses' request in two ways. He speaks about his attributes, which reveal what we may know about God (verses 19), and then he shows Moses his back (verses 20-23).

God's goodness: 'I will cause all my goodness to pass before you' (verse 19). The word 'goodness' is an umbrella term that covers several attributes especially those listed in Exodus

34:6-7: 'The Lord, the Lord, the compassionate and gracious God, slow to anger, abounding in love and faithfulness, maintaining love to thousands and forgiving wickedness, rebellion and sin.' We see these attributes exemplified in Christ's life on earth. He lived a holy life and then died for the wicked.

God's name: 'I will proclaim my name, the Lord, in your presence' (Exod. 33:19). The 'I AM THAT I AM' is the eternal and unchanging God who saw the affliction of his people and sent Moses to deliver them. He came from heaven to earth to redeem sinners. The Greek Old Testament (the Septuagint) translates 'Lord' as *kurios*, the word used in the Greek New Testament as a title for Jesus. He is 'the same yesterday and today and for ever' and one day every tongue will confess that Jesus Christ is Lord (Heb. 13:8; Phil. 2:10-11).

God's sovereignty: 'I will have mercy on whom I will have mercy, and I will have compassion on whom I will have compassion' (Exod. 33:19). God saves whoever he chooses. Paul cites these words in Romans 9:14 to answer those who think that the doctrine of election is unfair. God is sovereign – he saves some and hardens others, such as the Pharaoh at the time of the Exodus, because this is what God wanted to do. Salvation does not 'depend on man's desire or effort, but on God's mercy' (verse 16). God did not have to choose any, so how then can we accuse him of unfairness? We are in no position to argue against God our Maker (verses 19-29). Paul does not defend God but simply asserts that he loves and elects whom he wills, and he hates and reprobates whom he wills. However, the sovereign God forgives *everyone* who calls on him for pardon (Rom. 10:13). We call because we are chosen. Those who do not call are responsible for their choice even though that choice fulfils God's eternal plans, just as the wicked men who chose to crucify Christ carried out God's decree (Acts 2:23).

Moses sees God's back (Exod. 33:20-23)

Moses, watching from the entrance of the rock cave, glimpses only the back of God as he passes by. We see God's face and God's glory in the Lord Jesus Christ. Was John thinking of this incident in Moses' life when he wrote, 'The Word became flesh and dwelt among us, and we beheld His glory, the glory as of the only begotten of the Father, full of grace and truth'? Certainly, John's words four verses later recall Exodus 33:20: 'No one has seen God at any time. The only begotten Son, who is in the bosom of the Father, He has declared Him' (John 1:14,18, NKJV). When Philip asked a question similar to the one asked by Moses, 'Lord, show us the Father', Jesus replied, 'Anyone who has seen me has seen the Father ... Don't you believe that I am in the Father, and that the Father is in me? The words I say to you are not just my own. Rather, it is the Father, living in me, who is doing his work ... I am in the Father and the Father is in me' (John 14:8-11). Later the apostle Paul wrote that we see 'the glory of God in the face of Christ' (2 Cor. 4:6). In heaven, we will see more of this glory in answer to the Saviour's prayer: 'Father, I want those you have given me to be with me where I am, and to see my glory, the glory you have given me because you loved me before the creation of the world' (John 17:24).

Moses' radiant face (Exod. 34)

It is evident in Exodus 34 that Moses is speaking to someone whom he can see and whom he worships as God. Look for example at verses 5 and 8. 'The LORD came down in the cloud and stood there with him and proclaimed his name, the LORD ... Moses bowed to the ground at once and worshipped.'

Moses, now over the age of eighty, carries up Sinai two stone tablets on which God writes the Ten Commandments (verses 1,28). Moses prays, with the episode of the golden calf fresh in his thoughts, 'forgive our wickedness and our sin, and take us as your inheritance.' He is encouraged to pray for pardon because of God's declaration of his grace and love (verses 6-7).[12] How does God respond? 'I am making a covenant with you. Before all your people I will do wonders never before done in any nation in all the world. The people you live among will see how awesome is the work that I, the LORD, will do for you.' The 'wonders' include God's miraculous provision in the desert. However, there is a condition to the promise, 'Obey what I command you' (verses 9-11). The Lord spells out in verses 12-26 what it means to obey him. God especially commands his people to worship him alone because his name is the 'jealous God' (verse 14; 20:5). God compares himself to a husband who is jealous when his wife has an affair. Idolatry is spiritual adultery. Idolatry for the Jews took the shape of a golden calf; for us it is anyone or anything that makes us love Christ less.

What happened when Moses came down from Mount Sinai? The fear of the Israelites puzzled him until he realised that his face shone with God's glory. Moses put a veil over his face when he spoke to the people but removed this veil when he spoke to God (verses 29-35). It seems that this radiance faded until Moses went again into God's presence. What was the purpose of this radiance on Moses' face? To show that he spoke with God's authority. And why did he wear the veil? To calm the fear of the Israelites.

Paul unlocks the significance of Moses' shining face in 2 Corinthians 3:7-18.[13] We must take care with our exegesis of this passage. Paul is not comparing something bad with something good. Rather, the contrast is between the good and the better. The old covenant 'came with glory', but the new covenant is 'more glorious' (verses 7-8) because it 'brings righteousness' rather than condemnation (verse 9). The law condemns sinners. The gospel brings acquittal. The old 'was fading away', whereas the new 'lasts'. The old has served its purpose; nothing can replace the new (verses 11).

Paul contrasts himself to Moses in verses 12-13. Moses hid his face behind a veil so that the Israelites only occasionally saw it, unlike the apostle whose hearers could constantly see his face as he boldly preached the gospel. He was a man who was confident that his message would never become redundant, that the good news had power to change people's lives. The apostle draws another parallel in verses 14-16. Moses wore a piece of cloth over his face; now a veil of spiritual blindness covers the hearts of unbelievers. This explains why an unbelieving Jew who hears Messianic Scriptures read in a synagogue does not see their fulfilment in Christ. Likewise, regular unbelieving church-attenders listen to persuasive gospel preaching and remain unconverted.

Paul makes a further comparison between Christians and Jews in verses 17-18. The Lord sets believers free from the assumption that good deeds are the path to heaven. We have access into God's holy presence. As we spend time in his presence we desire to be like him and, in this way, we are gradually 'being transformed into his likeness with ever-increasing glory' (verse 18). We are to reflect the glory of the holy God by holy living.

God's glory fills the tabernacle (Exod. 40)

The statement in Exodus 40:34-35 that 'the glory of the LORD filled the tabernacle' parallels Exodus 24:16, where we read that 'the glory of the LORD settled on Mount Sinai.'

God dwelt on Sinai, separated from his people, whereas in the tabernacle he dwelt among them. God lived among his people as their guide and protector. How did he guide and protect them? By 'the cloud of the LORD' – when the cloud lifted, the Israelites moved camp. At night this cloud became a pillar of fire to defend God's people (Exod. 40:36-38).

We have in Exodus 40 what Currid calls 'the Immanuel principle'.[14] 'Immanuel' means 'God with us'. The prophet Isaiah predicts the coming of Immanuel into the world by a virgin birth: 'The virgin will be with child and will give birth to a son, and will call him Immanuel.' This same Person is the 'Wonderful Counsellor, Mighty God, Everlasting Father, Prince of Peace' (Isa. 7:14; 9:6). Matthew identifies him as Jesus, conceived by the Holy Spirit in the womb of a Jewish virgin named Mary, who is engaged to a carpenter named Joseph (Matt. 1:18-24).

Where does God live now that we have no special tent or temple? He lives, by his Holy Spirit, within the temple of his church. The Almighty God says, 'I will live with them and walk among them and I will be their God, and they will be my people' (1 Cor. 6:19-20; 2 Cor. 6:16). It is by his Holy Spirit that he guides and defends his people on their journey to heaven (Rom. 8:14).

We also read of God dwelling with his people in the final book of the Bible. 'I heard a loud voice from the throne saying, "Now the dwelling of God is with men, and he will live with them. They will be his people, and God himself will be with them and be their God."' What will happen when God lives with his people on the 'new earth'? 'He will wipe every tear from their eyes. There will be no more death or mourning or crying or pain' (Rev. 21:1-4).

Knowing Christ's invisible presence on earth we are 'filled with an inexpressible and glorious joy' – how much greater will be our joy when we 'see his face'! (1 Peter 1:8; Rev. 22:4).

Appendix 1.
Christ and Moses
(contrasts and comparsions)

A list of thirteen contrasts between Moses and Christ (without any comments) followed by eight comparisons between Moses and Christ linking references in Exodus to NT passages.

Before coming to the theme of Moses as a picture of Christ, we consider some of the striking contrasts in the life of Moses.

Contrasts
- He was a child of a slave, but son of a king
- He was born in a house, but he lived in a palace
- He was poor, but became wealthy
- He was a wealthy prince, but he became a poor shepherd
- He was educated in Egypt, but he lived in the desert
- He had the wisdom of Egypt, but the faith of a child
- He was the leader of people, but the meekest of men
- He was tempted with the pleasures of sin, but endured the pain of suffering
- He was slow in speech, but spoke with God
- He was a fugitive from Pharaoh, but an ambassador for God
- He died alone on a mountain, but appeared with Christ in Judea
- No man assisted at his funeral, but God buried him
- His lips are silent, but he still speaks

Comparisons with Christ

Do we have biblical warrant to see Moses as a picture of Christ? Indeed we do, in Deuteronomy 18:15 where we read, 'The LORD your God will raise up for you a prophet *like me* from among your own brothers. You must listen to him.' God spoke through Christ, the final prophet. 'In the past God spoke to our forefathers through the prophets … but in these last days he has spoken to us by his Son' (Heb. 1:1-2).

A.W. Pink uses six double-columned pages in small print to record seventy-five parallels between Moses and Christ.[1] We will pick up some of these parallels in this chapter.

1. Moses' birth and childhood

Moses was an Israelite (Exod. 2:1,2) and so was Christ. Moses' birth occurred when his nation was under the dominion of a hostile power (Exod. 1). The Jews were in bondage to the Romans when Christ was born in Bethlehem (Matt 2:1; Luke 24:21). Both Moses and Jesus faced danger as infants and lived as children in Egypt (Exod. 1:22; Matt 2:13; Hosea 11:1). Both Moses and Jesus spent their early years in obscurity – Moses in the desert and Jesus in Nazareth – before beginning their public work for God.

2. Moses' sympathy for his people

Moses felt deep compassion for his fellow-Hebrews and yearned for their deliverance (Exod. 2:11-15; Acts 7:23-24). Christ who 'loved the church and gave himself up for her', sympathizes with his tempted and tried people (Eph. 5:25; Heb. 2:18, 4:14-16). Just as Moses knew that God would use him to deliver Israel, so Jesus, even at the age of twelve, knew that he had come to earth on his 'Father's business' (Luke 2:49, AV). That business took him to the cross where he died in the place of his elect.

3. Moses' great renunciation

Moses' refusal 'to be known as the son of Pharaoh's daughter' and his deliberate choice 'to be ill-treated along with the people of God rather than to enjoy the pleasures of sin' anticipates Christ's act of humiliation (Heb 11:24-26; Phil. 2:5-8). The eternal God became a servant; he 'made himself nothing'. Men derided him as mad and demon-possessed. He chose to die on a cross, the symbol of rejection by men and by God (Gal. 3:13). Like Moses, he identified himself with God's people as he looked forward to his reward (Phil. 2:9-11; Heb. 12:2).

4. Moses the shepherd

Moses cared for the sheep of his father-in-law Jethro (Exod. 3:1). The Lord Jesus Christ said 'I am the good shepherd. The good shepherd lays down his life for the sheep ... My sheep listen to my voice; I know them, and they follow me. I give them eternal life, and they shall never perish; no-one can snatch them out of my hand. My Father, who has given them to me, is greater than all; no-one can snatch them out of my Father's hand' (John 10:11,27-29).

5. Moses performs miracles

Miracles confirmed to the Hebrews Moses' divine commission (Exod.

4:1-9,17,29-31). Likewise, Christ's miracles fulfilled prophecy, and thus authenticated his mission (Isa 35:4-6; Matt. 11:2-6). Moses is the first person in the Old Testament who performed miracles and Jesus Christ is the first in the New Testament to do miracles. John the Baptist pointed to Christ but never did any miracles himself (John 1:29,35-36).

God's miraculous provision of manna and quails, six days a week, for forty years and the water from the rock point forward to Christ, the bread and water for the soul (Exod. 16-17; John 4; 6; 7:37-39; 1 Cor. 10:1-6).

6. Moses prays

The Israelites grumbled against Moses and even wanted to stone him (Exod. 15:22-17:7) but he still loves the rebels. A striking example of his love for the Israelites comes after the incident of the golden calf (Exod. 32). 'Oh, what a great sin these people have committed! They have made for themselves gods of gold. But now, please forgive their sin – but if not, then blot me out of the book you have written', Moses prays (verses 31- 32). 'Punish me instead of the sinners' is the thrust of his prayer. God refuses to punish Moses because he too is a sinner. Only a perfect man can atone for sin. Christ alone, the sinless Son of God, could atone for sin. He bears the wrath of God his Father as he dies on the cross. While dying, he prays 'Father forgive them, for they do not know what they are doing.' Now in heaven, he prays for us, as our great high Priest and Advocate (Heb. 7:23-27).

At every crisis, Moses prays (see for example, Exod. 5:22; 8:12; 9:33; 15:25; 17:4). Jesus too, spent time in prayer and taught his disciples about prayer (see, for example, Mark 1:35; Matt. 6:5-14; Luke 11:1-13).

7. Moses' humility and obedience

We read that 'Moses was a very humble man, more humble than anyone else on the face of the earth' (Num. 12:3). Jesus said, 'Come to me, all you who are weary and burdened, and I will give you rest. Take my yoke upon you and learn from me, for I am gentle and humble in heart, and you will find rest for your souls. For my yoke is easy and my burden is light' (Matt. 11:28-30).

A refrain in the book of Exodus is 'Moses did everything just as the LORD commanded him.' Jesus said 'The one who sent me is with me; he has not left me alone, for I always do what pleases him' (Exod. 40:16; John 8:29).

8. Moses the prophet, priest and king

Moses is a prophet, priest and king to the Hebrews – a picture of Christ, the divine prophet, priest and king (Deut 18:18, Ps. 99:6; Lev. 8:15-16; Deut 33:4-5; Heb. 1:1-2, 4:14-5:8, 7:1- 8:13; Ps. 2; Luke 1:32-33).

Appendix 2.
Old Testament appearances of God – theophanies

Theophany means 'an appearance of God' and is derived from two Greek words 'theos' ('God') and 'phanein' ('to appear'). When Moses asked to see God's glory, the Lord replied, 'You cannot see my face, for no-one may see me and live.' Nevertheless, Moses was allowed to see God's back (Exod. 33:18,20-23). Besides Moses, other Old Testament people also saw God and lived, such as Abraham and Gideon. They saw a pre-incarnate appearance of Christ, God's Son; they saw God in Christ. At the burning bush, and on other occasions, Christ appeared as 'the angel of the LORD' – God's messenger – who is equal to God and yet a distinct Person of the Godhead. Sometimes these theophanies took a non-human form such as the Pillar of Cloud and Fire that guided God's people through the wilderness and the Shekinah Cloud that appeared over the tabernacle. This is a vast subject and scholars debate what constitutes a theophany, so I have not attempted to provide an exhaustive list of biblical references.

These appearances of God anticipate the incarnation and prepare us for the fuller revelation in the New Testament of Christ's deity and the doctrine of the Trinity. Theophanies ceased with the incarnation of the Lord Jesus Christ. Before the incarnation, Christ sometimes appeared in what *looked like* a human body; at the incarnation, he took a real human body with a real human nature. A theophany was temporary, the incarnation was permanent – even now, in heaven, Christ has a human nature and therefore feels for us when we suffer (Heb. 4:14-16). Replying to Philip's request, 'Show us the Father', Jesus said, 'Anyone who has seen me has seen the Father. How can you say, "Show us the Father"? Don't you believe that I am in the Father, and that the Father is in me? The words I say to you are not just my own. Rather, it is the Father, living in me, who is doing his work.' (John 14:8-10).

God appears in human form

To Abraham – Gen. 17:1; 18:1. The word 'appear' signifies 'to let oneself be seen.'[1]

To Jacob – Gen. 32:24-32. God wrestled with 'a man' but says 'I saw God face to face, and yet my life was spared' (verse 30).

To Moses – Exod. 33:18-23. Moses saw God's hand (verse 22) and his back (verse 23). See also Num. 12:8 – God speaking 'face to face' with Moses may imply a human form.

To Joshua – Josh. 5:13-6:5. The LORD appears as 'a man' who calls himself 'commander of the army of the LORD' (5:14).

Isaiah: Compare Isa. 6:1 with John 12:37-41. See also Isa. 63:9.

Shadrach, Meshach, Abednego and Daniel: Dan. 3:25,28; 6:21-22; 8:15-18 (Daniel 'was terrified and fell prostrate' in the presence of 'one like a man'); 7:21-22 ('The Ancient of Days … The Most High) 10:5-12,18; 12:5-13.

'The angel of the LORD'

Hagar: Gen. 16:1-16. She calls 'the angel of the LORD' 'the God who sees me' (verse 13).

Abraham: Gen. 22:11.

Moses: Exod. 3:2; 14:19; 23:20; 32:34. Cf. 33:2.

Balaam; Num. 22:21-35.

The Israelites: Judg. 2:1-4.

Gideon: Judg. 6:11-23. 'The angel of the LORD' is called 'LORD' (Jehovah) in several verses, for example, verses 14, 16 and 23. Gideon declares 'Ah, Sovereign LORD! I have seen the angel of the LORD face to face!' (verse 22) and the LORD responds by assuring him that nevertheless he will not die (verse 23).

Manoah and his wife (parents of Samson): Judg. 13:1-25 – 'A man of God' (verse 6) is identified as 'the angel of the LORD' (verse 3). Manoah then says to his wife, 'we have seen God!' (verse 22).

David: 2 Sam. 24:15-17 (note verse 16) and 1 Chr. 21:14-18 (note verse 15).

Elijah: 1 Kings 19:9-18. Elijah hears God – and possibly saw him – in 'a gentle whisper' (verse 12). In 2 Kings 1:3,15, we read that 'The angel of the LORD' spoke to the prophet. Cf. 2 Kings 6:17 and 19:35 where we read that 'the angel of the LORD' delivered Hezekiah from Sennacherib the king of Assyria.

Zechariah: Zech. 1:11-12; 3:5; 12:8. Cf. Zech. 2:1-5 and 4:1.

We also read about 'The angel of the LORD' in Ps. 34:7 and 35:5-6.

Further appearances of God

It is not always clear what people saw when God spoke or revealed himself but the following suggest some sort of physical appearance.

Gen. 2:15-16,22: 'The LORD God took the man and put him in the Garden' (verse 15) and 'The LORD God made a woman … and he brought her to the man' (verse 22).

Gen. 3:8-19,21: God spoke to Adam and Eve and walked in the Garden (verse 8). The Creator speaks to sinful Adam and Eve and to the serpent (verses 9-19). God clothes Adam and Eve (verse 21).

Gen.5:22,24; 6:9: 'Enoch walked with God'; 'Noah walked with God'.

Genesis chapters 6-9: '[There] are thirty-nine verses which contain a monologue of instruction from God to Noah and his three sons.'[2]

Gen. 12:1-3,7. Cf. Acts 7:2-3, 'The God of glory appeared to our father Abraham while he was still in Mesopotamia.' See also John 8:56.

Exod. 24:9-10: The seventy elders *saw* the God of Israel who 'did not raise his hand against these leaders of the Israelites; they saw God, and they ate and drank.' Moses tells us about God's surroundings – his sapphire throne – but how they saw God is not recorded.

1 Sam. 3:10: 'The LORD came and stood there, calling as at the other times, "Samuel! Samuel!"' Did Samuel see Christ in human form?

To Job: Job 38-42. Note 42:5, 'Now my eyes have seen you.'

Ezekiel: Ezk.1 and 10. The prophet 'saw visions of God' (1:1) and 'the glory of the LORD' (10:4).

Further reading

The book of Exodus

Michael Bentley, *Travelling Homeward – Exodus simply explained* (Welwyn Commentary). Evangelical Press, 1999.

John D. Currid, *Exodus Volume 1* (Chapters 1-18), *Volume 2* (Chapters 19-40). An Evangelical Press study commentary, 2000 and 2001. Both Bentley and Currid are sound expositors with helpful application.

John J. Davis, *Moses and the gods of Egypt – studies in Exodus.* Baker Book House, 1971.Davis relates the events in the book of Exodus to their historical and political context. His treatment of the Tabernacle is excellent.

The life of Moses

Roger Ellsworth, *Moses – God's man for challenging times.* Evangelical Press, 2005. Ellsworth is a prolific author who is always readable.

The Ten Commandments

Brian Edwards, *The Ten Commandments for today.* Day One Publications, 1996.

Peter Masters, *God's rules for holiness – unlocking The Ten Commandments.* The Wakeman Trust, 2003.

Christ in the Old Testament

Edgar Andrews, *Preaching Christ* (ET perspectives series), Evangelical Times, 2005.

James Borland, *Christ in the Old Testament*, Moody Press, Chicago, 1978.

A useful commentary series

I recommend the Welwyn Commentary Series. For a list of titles go to www.epbooks.org.

Recommended Bible Notes

Geneva Bible Reading Notes, Grace Publications, every three months. For details see www.gracepublications.co.uk

References

Quoting an author does not mean that I necessarily agree with everything he has written!

Chapter 1. Christ in all the Scriptures

1. Henry Shires, cited by Graeme Goldsworthy, *Gospel and Kingdom – A Christian Interpretation of The Old Testament*, Paternoster Press, 1981, p. 19.
2. Peter Masters, *Not like any other Book – Interpreting the Bible*, Wakeman Trust, London, 2004, pp. 20-21.
3. See also Mark 12:26; Luke 20:37; John 5:46,47; 7:22,23.
4. Roger Ellsworth, *The Guide – The Bible Book by Book*, Evangelical Press, 2002, p. 16.
5. Ellsworth, *The Guide*, p. 16.
6. Robert J. Sheehan, *The Word of Truth*, Evangelical Press, p. 43.
7. Michael Bentley, *Travelling Homewards – Exodus simply explained* (Welwyn Commentary), Evangelical Press, 1999, p. 14.
8. John Murray, *Redemption Accomplished and Applied*, Banner of Truth, 1961, pp. 42-43.
9. Philip Eveson, *Understanding Redemption from Exodus*, The Evangelical Magazine of Wales, June/July 2000, pp. 10-11.
10. Eveson, p. 11.
11. See also Acts 7:44 and Hebrews 8:5.
12. Masters, p. 2 [footnote].

Chapter 2. Christ the Redeemer (Exod. 1-3)

1. Bentley, p. 30.
2. Bentley, p. 31.
3. J. Philip Arthur, *No Turning Back – an exposition of Hebrews*, Grace Publications, 2003, p. 188.

4. Bentley, p. 36.
5. William Hendriksen, *New Testament Commentary – The Gospel of Luke*, Banner of Truth, 1978, pp. 180,186 (Hendriksen's italics).
6. Hendriksen, *New Testament Commentary* – Philippians, Banner of Truth, 1962, p. 108.

Chapter 3. Christ is Lord (Exod. 3)

1. Bentley, pp. 57-58.
2. John D. Currid, *Exodus Volume 1 Chapters 1-18* (An EP Study Commentary), Evangelical Press, 2000.
3. Bentley, p. 59, p. 80.
4. See also Exod. 13:21, 14:24, 19:18. Compare 1 John 1:5 and 1 Tim. 6:16.
5. See Appendix 2, 'Old Testament appearances of God – theophanies.'
6. In Exodus 33:2, we read about 'an angel' rather than 'my angel' as in 32:34 or 'the angel' as in 3:2.
7. Robert J. Sheehan, *The Word of Truth*, Evangelical Press, 1998, p. 40.
8. Sheehan, p. 41.
9. Herman Bavinck *The Doctrine of God*, Banner of Truth, 1977, p.106.
10. Bentley, p. 65.
11. Currid, Volume 1, p. 137.
12. Gordon J. Keddie, *John Volume 1 Chapters 1-12*, (An EP Study Commentary), Evangelical Press, 2001, p. 363.
13. Henry Mahan, *Bible Class Commentary – John*, Evangelical Press, 1987, p. 2.
14. Keddie, Volume 1, p. 262.
15. Keddie, Volume 1, p. 322.
16. Keddie, *John Volume 2, Chapters 13-21*, (An EP Study Commentary). Evangelical Press, 2001, pp. 95-96.

Chapter 4. Christ the Messiah (Exod. 3-11)

1. Currid, Volume 1, p. 89.
2. Richard Brooks, *The Lamb is all the glory – the book of Revelation* (Welwyn Commentary), Evangelical Press, 1986, p. 176.
3. Currid, Volume 1, p. 113.
4. Currid, Volume 1, p. 155.
5. Bentley, p. 76.

Chapter 5. Christ the Passover Lamb (Exod. 12)

1. Henry Law, *The Gospel in Exodus*, Banner of Truth reprint, 1967, p. 23.
2. Jamieson-Faussett-Brown, *Commentary on the whole Bible*, QuickVerse 8 Bible Software, A division of Findex, Inc, Omaha, Nebraska, USA.
3. John Davis, *Moses and the gods of Egypt*, Baker Book House, 1971, p. 150.
4. Charles Hodge, *Commentary on 1st Corinthians*, Banner of Truth reprint, 1958, p. 87.

Chapter 6. Christ the Saviour (Exod. 14)

1. Arthur, p. 192.
2. Arthur, p. 193.
3. John MacArthur, *Commentary on 1 Corinthians*, Moody Press, Chicago, 1984, p. 218.
4. Roger Ellsworth, *Strengthening Christ's Church – the message of 1 Corinthians simply explained* (Welwyn Commentary), Evangelical Press. 1995, p. 159.
5. MacArthur, p. 220.
6. Currid, Volume 1, pp. 283-4.
7. Currid, Volume 1, p. 300.

Chapter 7. Christ the True Bread (Exod. 16)

1. William Gurnall, *The Christian in Complete Armour, Volume 1*, A modernized abridgement of the 1864 edition by Ruthanne Galrock, Kay King, Karen Sloan and Candy Coan, Banner of Truth, 1986, p. 25.
2. Currid, Volume 1, p. 341.
3. Currid, Volume 1, p. 283.
4. Keil and Delitzsch, *Commentary on the Old Testament Volume 1*, QuickVerse 8 Bible Software.
5. Henry Mahan, *Bible Class Commentary – John*, Evangelical Press, 1987, p. 62.
6. Mahan, p. 66
7. Charles Caldwell Ryrie, *The Ryrie Study Bible* – note on Revelation 2:17. Moody Press, Chicago, 1985.
8. Richard Brooks, *The Lamb is all the glory – the book of Revelation* (Welwyn Commentary), Evangelical Press, 1986, p. 38.

Chapter 8. Christ the Rock (Exod. 17)

1. Keil and Delitzsch, *Commentary on the Old Testament Volume 1*, QuickVerse 8 Bible Software.
2. Keil and Delitzsch.
3. Currid, Volume 1, p. 361
4. Currid, Volume 1, p. 362
5. Bentley, p. 207.
6. John MacArthur, *1 Corinthians*, Moody Press, 1984, p. 220.
7. Stuart Olyott, *Dare to stand alone* (Welwyn Commentary on Daniel), Evangelical Press, 1982, p. 33.
8. Hendriksen, *New Testament Commentary – the Gospel of John*, Volume 1. Banner of Truth, 1964, p. 162.
9. Hendriksen, *John* Volume 2, p. 26

Chapter 9. Christ gives rest (Exod. 17-18)

1. Arthur, p. 63.
2. Edgar Andrews, *A glorious high throne – Hebrews simply explained* (Welwyn Commentary), Evangelical Press, 2003, p. 104.
3. Andrews, p. 118.
4. Andrews, p. 119.
5. Andrews, p. 123.
6. Arthur, pp. 70-71.
7. J. C. Ryle, *Expository Thoughts on Matthew*, James Clarke, 1974 reprint, p. 120.

Chapter 10. Christ fulfils the law (Exod. 20)

1. Hendriksen, *New Testament Commentary – The Gospel of Mark*, Banner of Truth, 1976. p. 393
2. Hendriksen, *New Testament Commentary – The Gospel of Matthew*, Banner of Truth, 1974, pp. 287.
3. Hendriksen, *Matthew*, p. 291.
4. The AV translation, 'the law was our schoolmaster', translated as 'tutor' in the NKJV, is misleading because Christ, not the law, is our teacher.
5. Currid discusses this question in 'Appendix 2: The law of God and the church today', in *Exodus Volume 2 Chapters 19-40* (An EP Study Commentary), Evangelical Press, 2001, pp. 376-382.
6. Dr. Martyn Lloyd-Jones, *The Sermon on the Mount Volume 1*, Inter Varsity Fellowship, 1959, pp. 16-17.

7. Brian Edwards, *The Ten Commandments for today*, Day One Publications, 1996, p. 38. Edwards presents the reasons why the Commandments apply to all nations and are the rule of obedience for Christians.
8. See chapter 3, 'Christ is Lord.'
9. Archibald Thomas Robertson, *Word Pictures in the New Testament, Volume 1, Matthew and Mark*, QuickVerse 8 Bible Software.
10. Edwards, p. 41.
11. 1 Cor. 15:45.
12. Hendriksen, *New Testament Commentary – Galatians*, Banner of Truth, 1969, pp. 130-131 (Hendriksen's italics).
13. Bentley, p. 232 (Bentley's italics).
14. Arthur, p. 218.
15. Stuart Olyott, *The Gospel as it really is – Romans simply explained* (Welwyn Commentary), Evangelical Press, 1979, p. 91. For a fuller discussion of Romans 10:4 and the meaning of the word 'end' read John Murray, *The Epistle to the Romans* (New International Commentary on the New Testament), pp. 48-49. Wm B Eerdmans Publishing Company Co. Grand Rapids, Michigan, 1968.
16. Hendriksen, *Matthew*, p. 810.

Chapter 11. Christ the Servant (Exod. 21)

1. Brian Edwards has written an excellent biography of John Newton, *Through many dangers – the story of John Newton*, published by Evangelical Press.
2. Harry Uprichard, *A Son is promised – Christ in the Psalms*, Evangelical Press, 1994, pp. 98-99.
3. Hendriksen, *New Testament Commentary – the Gospel of John*, Banner of Truth, 1959, pp. 70-71.
4. Charles Wesley, *Let earth and heaven combine*, Christian Hymns, 174 (1977 edition).
5. James Murphy, *A critical and exegetical commentary on the book of Exodus*, T & T Clarke, 1866, p.235.
6. Francis Ridley Havergal, *Redemption Hymnal* 542. Elim Publishing House, Eastbourne, Sussex, 1951.

Chapter 12. Christ the Tabernacle (Exod. 25 etc)

1. Davis, p. 257. Davis shows sketches of the possible shapes of the tabernacle.
2. Davis, p. 268.

3. Davis, pp. 257-261.
4. Davis, pp. 268-269.
5. Bentley, p. 276.
6. Gordon J. Keddie, *According to Promise – the message of the book of Numbers*, (Welwyn Commentary), Evangelical Press, 1992, p. 22. There is a useful plan showing the encampment of Israel around the tabernacle on page 23.
7. Davis, p. 272.
8. Bentley, p. 280.
9. Frederick S. Leahy, *Is it nothing to you? The unchanging significance of the cross*. Banner of Truth, 2004, pp. 108-109. Leahy's information concerning the size of the veil comes from the Misnach (Jewish oral tradition). Chapter 9, *The sign of the Rent Veil* is excellent; indeed, the whole book of 134 pages is recommended for its fresh insights into Christ's sufferings.
10. Leahy, pp. 107-108,111.
11. Merrill F. Unger, cited by Davis, p. 264.
12. Simon J. Kistemaker, *New Testament Commentary: Hebrews*, Evangelical Press, 1984, p. 240.
13. F. F. Bruce, *Commentary on the Epistle to the Hebrews*, Marshall, Morgan and Scott, 1964, p. 190.
14. Hendriksen, *New Testament Commentary – Romans 1-8*, Banner of Truth, 1980, p. 123.
15. See my Welwyn Commentary, *Doing a great work – Ezra and Nehemiah simply explained*, Evangelical Press, 1996.
16. Herman Hoeksema, *Behold He cometh – an exposition of the Book of Revelation*, Reformed Free Publishing Association, Grand Rapids, Michigan, 1969, p. 674.

Chapter 13. Christ the great High Priest (Exod. 28-29)

1. Masters, *Interpreting the Bible*, p21 [footnote].
2. For a summary of the priest's duties see Davis, pp. 281-282.
3. *Collins Concise Dictionary*.
4. Bentley, p. 288.
5. I suggest in my Welwyn commentary, *Doing a great work – Ezra and Nehemiah simply explained*, Evangelical Press, 1996, that the Urim and Thummim may have 'comprised two stones … which lit up to indicate God's will when faced with alternative actions' (p. 29). I'm less convinced of that view now! Davis discusses the various suggestions concerning these mysterious objects on pages 285-287. Other biblical references to the Urim and Thummim are Lev. 8:8; Num. 27:21; Deut. 33:8; 1 Sam. 28:6; Ezra 2:63 and Neh. 7:65.

6. Bentley, p. 288.
7. Davis, p. 287.
8. Henry Law, *The Gospel in Exodus*, p. 136. Banner of Truth reprint 1967.
9. Currid, Volume 2, p. 208.
10. Currid, Volume 2, p. 208.
11. Currid, Volume 2, p. 211.
12. Davis, p. 283

Chapter 14. Christ the Mediator (Exod. 32)

1. Davis, p. 291.
2. John MacArthur, *Commentary on 1 Corinthians*, p. 223. Moody Press, Chicago, 1984.
3. Bentley, p. 319.
4. See chapter 3, Christ is Lord.
5. Bentley, p. 317.
6. Currid, Volume 2, pp. 276-277.
7. Hendriksen, *New Testament Commentary – the Gospel of Luke*, p. 735. Banner of Truth, 1978.
8. A similar sentiment is expressed by the apostle Paul in Romans 9:1-3.
9. Keil and Delitzsch, *Commentary on Old Testament, Volume 1.* QuickVerse 8 Bible Software.
10. See chapter 3, Christ is Lord.
11. Bentley, p. 320.
12. Bentley, p. 325.

Chapter 15. Christ the Shekinah glory (Exod. 24, 33, 34, 40).

1. See for example Exod. 2:24-25; Deut 33:27; Ps. 17:1-2,4,6,8,14,15; Psalm 34:15-17 and Isa. 59:1-2. The theological term for attributing human characteristics to God is anthropomorphism.
2. Currid, Volume 1, p. 300.
3. Holman's Bible Dictionary. QuickVerse 8 Bible Software.
4. Currid, Volume 2, p. 138; compare Isa. 6 with John 12:37-41. See also Revelation 4 and 5. Bentley asserts that Moses, and his companions, saw 'merely a reflection of God's glory', p. 265. Davis comments, 'Whatever the precise nature of the vision, it was majestic and served to illustrate the power of God who had given the revelation', p. 250.
5. Currid, Volume 2, pp. 138-9.

6. Exodus 32. See chapter 13, Christ the Mediator.
7. Compare Heb. 3:1-6. See chapter 9, Christ gives rest.
8. 'It was the Deity manifesting Himself so as to be cognizable to mortal eye' (Albert Barnes). Moses saw 'some unmistakable evidence of His glorious presence' (Jamieson, Faussett, Brown). Quotes taken from QuickVerse 8 Bible Software.
9. Our understanding of 'face to face' in 1 Cor. 13:12 depends on how we interpret 'when perfection comes' in verse 10. Peter Naylor argues that the 'perfection' refers to the Scriptures, whereas John MacArthur and Roger Ellsworth see the 'perfection' as heaven. To quote Ellsworth, Paul 'is talking about the coming of the perfect age or the coming of our perfect life in heaven'. In this view he is following in the footsteps of older commentators such as Albert Barnes and Charles Hodge (See *1 Corinthians*, Naylor; *Strengthening Christ's Church*, Ellsworth – both published by Evangelical Press, and *1 Corinthians*, John MacArthur, published by Moody Press).
10. Keil and Delitzsch, Volume 1.
11. See chapter 3, Christ is Lord, and Exod. 14:19; 23:20; 32:34; 33:2.
12. God's words in Exodus 34:6-7 are quoted several times in the Bible, see for example, Num. 14:18; Neh. 9:17; Ps. 86:15; Ps. 103:8; Ps. 145:8; Joel 2:13 and Jonah 4:2.
13. For a more detailed exposition of this passage read J. Philip Arthur, *Strength in weakness – 2 Corinthians simply explained* (Welwyn Commentary), Evangelical Press, 2004, pp. 73-85.
14. Currid, Volume 2, p. 369.

Appendix 1. Christ and Moses

1. A. W. Pink, *Gleanings in Exodus,* Moody Press, Chicago, 1972, chapter 72, pp. 379-384.

Appendix 2. Old Testament appearances of God – theophanies

1. James Borland, *Christ in the Old Testament*, Moody Press, Chicago, 1978, p. 77.
2. Borland, p. 89.